CALIFORNIA TEST PREP
Smarter Balanced Practice
SBAC Mathematics
Grade 3

© 2018 by C. Hawas

All rights reserved. No part of this book may be reproduced or transmitted in any form or by any means, electronic, mechanical, photocopying, recording, or otherwise without prior written permission.

ISBN 978-1726093286

TEST MASTER PRESS

www.testmasterpress.com

CONTENTS

Introduction   4

45-Minute Introductory Tests   5
   Practice Set 1   5
   Practice Set 2   13

60-Minute Practice Tests   21
   Practice Set 3   21
   Practice Set 4   33
   Practice Set 5   46
   Practice Set 6   58
   Practice Set 7   70
   Practice Set 8   82
   Practice Set 9   94
   Practice Set 10   106

Answer Key   121
   Practice Set 1   122
   Practice Set 2   124
   Practice Set 3   125
   Practice Set 4   127
   Practice Set 5   129
   Practice Set 6   130
   Practice Set 7   131
   Practice Set 8   133
   Practice Set 9   134
   Practice Set 10   135

INTRODUCTION
For Parents, Teachers, and Tutors

About the Common Core State Standards

The state of California has adopted the Common Core State Standards. These standards describe the skills that students are expected to have. Student learning throughout the year is based on these standards, and all the questions on the state tests assess these standards. Just like the real state tests, the questions in this book assess whether students have the knowledge and skills described in the Common Core State Standards.

About the Smarter Balanced Assessments

In the 2014-2015 school year, the state of California introduced new assessments. These are the Smarter Balanced, or the SBAC, assessments. This book contains ten practice sets that will help prepare students for the Smarter Balanced assessments. The practice sets cover all the Common Core skills assessed and provide practice with the types of questions and tasks found on the real assessments.

Types of Questions on the Smarter Balanced Assessments

The Smarter Balanced Assessments are taken online and include a wider range of question formats than previous tests. The question types found on the test are summarized below.

- Selected-response (single answer) - students select the one correct answer from four possible options.
- Selected-response (multiple answers) - students select one or more correct answers.
- Constructed-response - students provide a numerical or a text answer. These tasks may involve providing a simple numerical answer, filling in a blank, completing a missing number in an expression, completing numbers in a table, or writing either a simple text answer or a more advanced text answer that explains a mathematical concept or explains mathematical thinking.
- Technology-enhanced - students use online features to complete a task. These tasks may involve sorting items into groups, placing items in order, using fraction models, drawing shapes, plotting points on a number line or grid, or completing graphs and charts.
- Performance tasks - these are extended tasks that are completed in combination with a classroom activity and involve completing a number of related questions. The question formats are the same as those above. While the performance tasks are not the focus of this book, gaining experience with all the question types will help prepare students for the tasks.

This book contains a wide range of question types, including questions that mimic the formats that use online features. By completing the practice sets, students will develop all the Common Core skills they need and become familiar with all the question types they will encounter on the real Smarter Balanced assessments.

Taking the Tests

The first two practice sets introduce students to the assessments with 10 questions that cover all the common question types. These short tests will allow students to become familiar with Smarter Balanced questions before moving on to longer tests. These shorter tests may also be used as guided instruction before allowing students to complete the assessments on their own. The remaining practice sets each have 20 questions. Students will have an experience similar to the real assessments, but with fewer questions and a shorter test length. By completing the practice sets, students will have ongoing practice with assessment items, develop the Common Core math skills they need, gain experience with all types of test questions, and become comfortable with the Smarter Balanced assessments.

SBAC Mathematics

Grade 3

Practice Set 1

Instructions

Read each question carefully. For each multiple-choice question, fill in the circle for the correct answer. For other types of questions, follow the directions given in the question.

You may use a ruler to help you answer questions. You may not use a calculator on this test.

This test should take 45 minutes to complete.

1   Which fraction is represented by point Y?

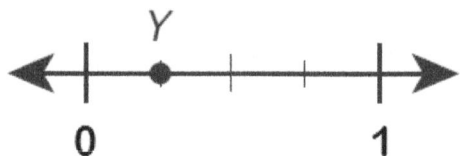

- Ⓐ $\frac{1}{3}$
- Ⓑ $\frac{1}{4}$
- Ⓒ $\frac{1}{5}$
- Ⓓ $\frac{1}{8}$

2   Sandra started walking to school at 8:45 a.m. It took her 25 minutes to get to school. What time did she get to school?

- Ⓐ 9:00 a.m.
- Ⓑ 9:10 a.m.
- Ⓒ 9:15 a.m.
- Ⓓ 9:20 a.m.

3 Karisa wants to determine how much water the dog bowl below can hold. Which measurement would Karisa be best to find?

- Ⓐ Volume
- Ⓑ Weight
- Ⓒ Height
- Ⓓ Length

4 Morgan earns money on the weekend by washing cars. He washed 4 cars for $8 each. He was also given a tip of $5 by one customer. How much money did Morgan make in all? Write an expression below to show how much Morgan made, in dollars. Then simplify the expression to find how much Morgan made, in dollars.

Expression _____

Answer _____

5   Select **all** the equations that will be true if the number 8 is placed in the empty box.

☐   6 × ☐ = 48

☐   8 × ☐ = 56

☐   9 × ☐ = 72

☐   24 ÷ ☐ = 4

☐   40 ÷ ☐ = 5

☐   64 ÷ ☐ = 8

6   Plot the four fractions listed below on the number line.

$$\frac{3}{4} \quad \frac{6}{3} \quad \frac{4}{4} \quad \frac{3}{1}$$

7   Sam kept a record of the types of movies each customer in his store rented. Sam made the table below to show the results.

Type of Movie	Number of Rentals
Action	12
Comedy	14
Drama	8
Science fiction	18

Use the information in the table to complete the graph below.

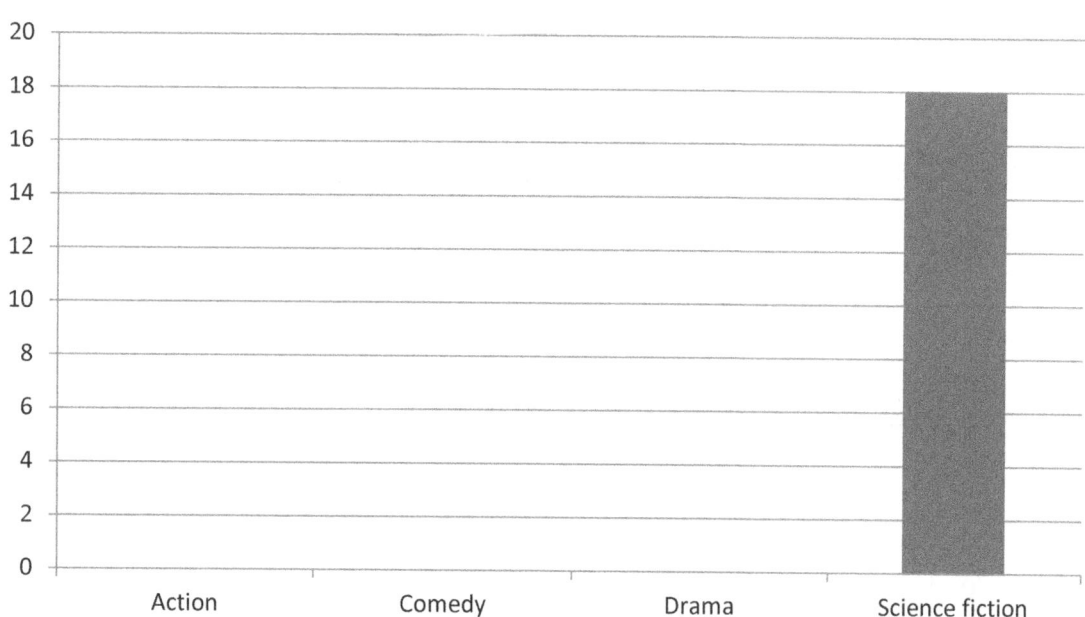

Number of Movie Rentals

8   Hannah sorts the figures below into those that are parallelograms and those that are not parallelograms.

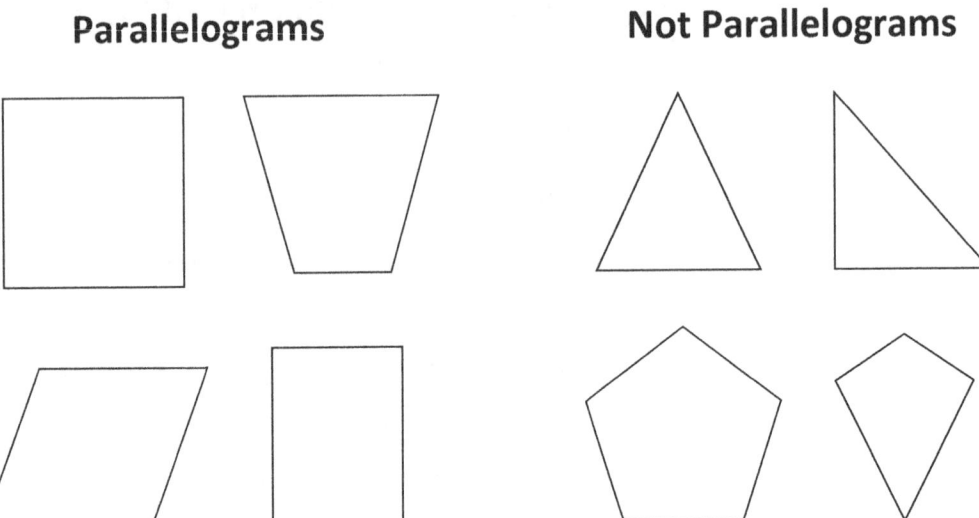

Circle the shape above that Hannah has sorted incorrectly. On the lines below, explain why the shape is sorted incorrectly.

_____

_____

_____

_____

_____

9 Emilio wants to create a vegetable garden with the shape shown below. On the diagram below, write the numbers in the boxes to show the missing dimensions.

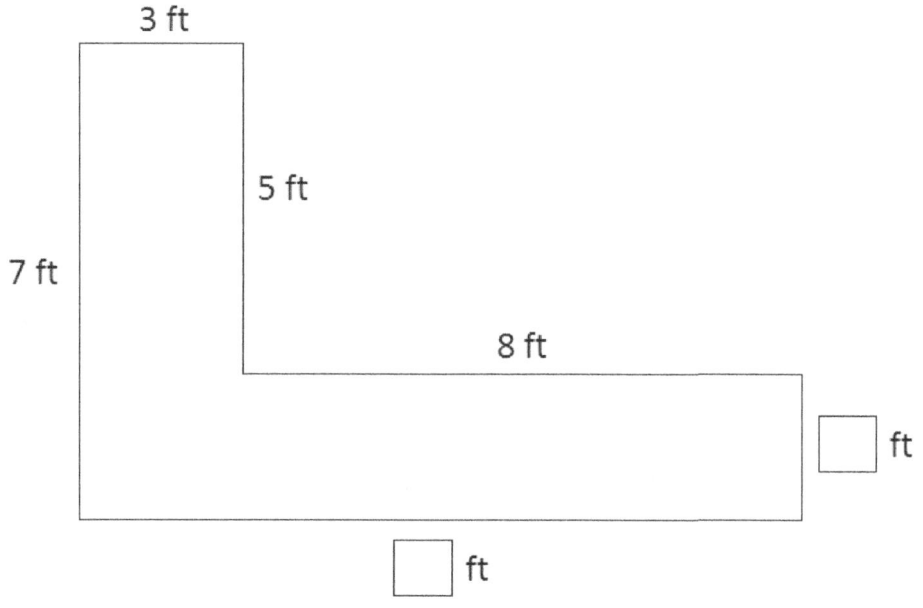

Draw a line on the diagram to divide it into two rectangles. Find the total area of the garden. Write your answer below.

_____ square feet

Find the perimeter of the garden. Write your answer below.

_____ feet

10 Craig draws the rectangle below. Craig states that all rectangles with an area of 12 square units have a perimeter of 14 units. On the grid above, draw a second rectangle that shows that Craig is incorrect.

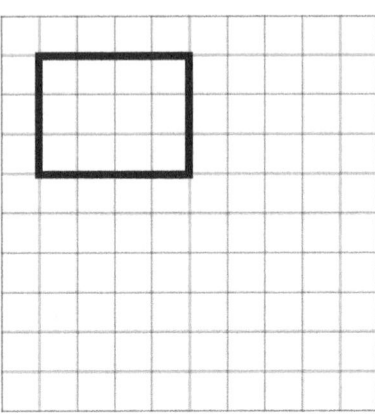

On the lines below, explain how you can tell that Craig is incorrect.

_____

_____

_____

_____

END OF PRACTICE SET

SBAC Mathematics

Grade 3

Practice Set 2

Instructions

Read each question carefully. For each multiple-choice question, fill in the circle for the correct answer. For other types of questions, follow the directions given in the question.

You may use a ruler to help you answer questions. You may not use a calculator on this test.

This test should take 45 minutes to complete.

1   Ryan's basketball team scored 74 points in a match. The team won the match by 9 points. How many points did the other team score?

   Ⓐ 81

   Ⓑ 83

   Ⓒ 65

   Ⓓ 67

2   Andy is learning to speak French. Andy learns 5 new words every day. Complete the table below to show how many words Andy has learned in all after each day.

Number of Days	Number of Words Learned
1	
2	
3	
4	
5	

3   Anton looked at the clock below.

Which of the following is closest to the time shown on the clock?

Ⓐ   6:20

Ⓑ   4:30

Ⓒ   4:45

Ⓓ   9:00

4   What is the length of the nail shown below? Write your answer below.

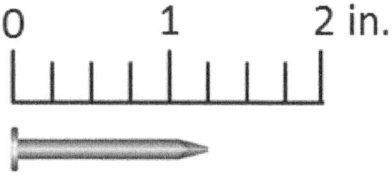

_____ inches

5 Select **all** the fractions that are equivalent to the shaded area of the circle below.

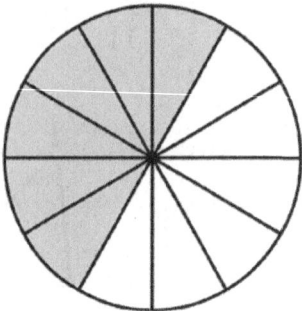

☐ $\frac{6}{1}$

☐ $\frac{1}{2}$

☐ $\frac{6}{12}$

☐ $\frac{2}{4}$

☐ $\frac{8}{4}$

☐ $\frac{2}{3}$

6 Jo has 18 star-shaped stickers. He places them in 3 even rows. Which of these shows how many stickers are in each row?

Ⓐ

Ⓑ

Ⓒ

Ⓓ

7 Simon had $896 in his savings account. He spent $179 on car repairs. How much money does Simon have left? Write your answer below.

$ _____

8 Alex started the number pattern below. Continue the pattern by writing the next four numbers on the lines below.

6, 10, 14, 18, 22, _____, _____, _____, _____

Will all the numbers in the pattern be even? Explain why or why not.

_____

_____

_____

_____

9 The pictograph below shows how long Tammy spent at the computer each week day.

Monday	🖥🖥🖥🖥
Tuesday	🖥🖥🖥🖥🖥🖥
Wednesday	🖥🖥🖥🖥🖥
Thursday	🖥🖥🖥
Friday	🖥🖥

Each 🖥 means 10 minutes.

On which day did Tammy spend the least time at the computer? Write your answer below.

_____

How many minutes did Tammy spend at the computer on Monday? Write your answer below.

_____ minutes

How much more time did Tammy spend at the computer on Tuesday than Thursday? Write your answer below.

_____ minutes

10 Look at the shaded figure below.

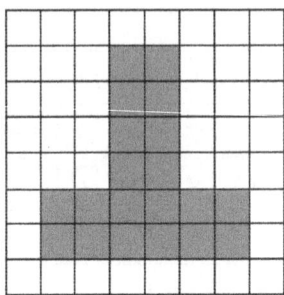

Divide the figure into two rectangles. Write the dimensions of the two rectangles below.

Rectangle 1: _____ by _____ units

Rectangle 2: _____ by _____ units

What is the total area of the shaded figure? Write your answer below.

_____ square units

END OF PRACTICE SET

SBAC Mathematics

Grade 3

Practice Set 3

Instructions

Read each question carefully. For each multiple-choice question, fill in the circle for the correct answer. For other types of questions, follow the directions given in the question.

You may use a ruler to help you answer questions. You may not use a calculator on this test.

This test should take 60 minutes to complete.

1 Mario buys screws in packets of 6.

If Mario counts the screws in groups of 6, which of these numbers would he count? Circle **all** the numbers he would count.

| 16 | 18 | 22 | 26 |

| 30 | 36 | 40 | 42 |

2 The graph shows how long Jason studied for one week.

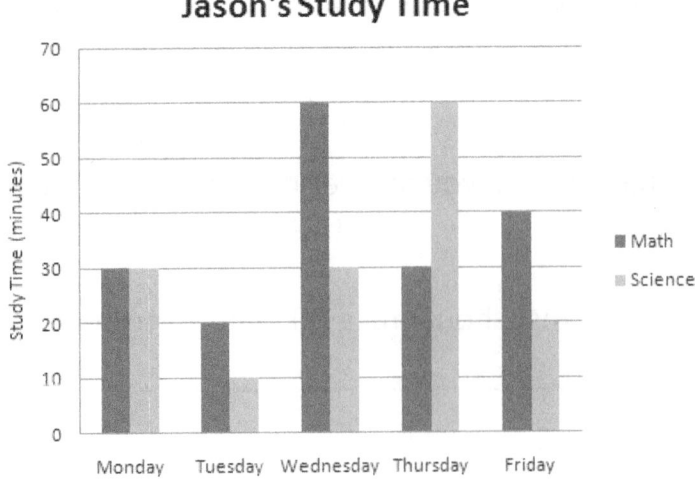

On what day did Jason study science for 30 minutes less than math? Write your answer below.

_____

3   Select **all** the fractions below that are equal to 4.

☐ $\frac{2}{8}$

☐ $\frac{8}{4}$

☐ $\frac{15}{5}$

☐ $\frac{4}{1}$

☐ $\frac{12}{3}$

4   Sally is making a pictograph to show how many students are in grade 3, grade 4, and grade 5.

Grade 3	☺☺☺☺☺☺☺☺☺☺
Grade 4	☺☺☺☺☺☺☺☺☺☺☺☺
Grade 5	

☺ = 5 students

There are 65 students in grade 5. Which of these should Sally use to represent 65 students?

Ⓐ   ☺☺☺☺☺☺☺☺☺☺☺

Ⓑ   ☺☺☺☺☺☺☺☺☺☺☺☺

Ⓒ   ☺☺☺☺☺☺☺☺☺☺☺☺☺

Ⓓ   ☺☺☺☺☺☺☺☺☺☺☺☺☺☺

5 Damon rode 3 miles to school every morning, and 3 miles back home each afternoon. How many miles would he ride in 5 days?

- Ⓐ 15 miles
- Ⓑ 30 miles
- Ⓒ 45 miles
- Ⓓ 60 miles

6 Ribbon costs $4 per yard. Allie buys 16 yards of ribbon. Which number sentence could be used to find the total cost of the ribbon, *c*, in dollars?

- Ⓐ $16 + 4 = c$
- Ⓑ $16 - 4 = c$
- Ⓒ $16 \times 4 = c$
- Ⓓ $16 \div 4 = c$

7 Allen's car has traveled 25,648 miles since it was new. What is this number rounded to the nearest hundred? Write your answer below.

_____

8 The school library has 1,532 fiction books, 1,609 non-fiction books, and 1,239 children's books. Complete the number sentence by rounding each number to the nearest hundred and then completing the addition.

1,500 + _____ + _____ = _____

9 There are 157 male students and 165 female students at Ella's school. How many students are there in all?

Ⓐ 322

Ⓑ 312

Ⓒ 222

Ⓓ 212

10 Plot the fraction $1\frac{1}{4}$ on the number line below.

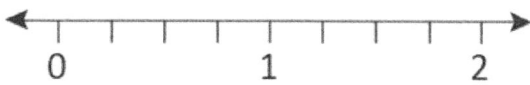

11 Look at the group of numbers below. Round each number to the nearest ten. Write your answers below.

108 _____ 864 _____

87 _____ 196 _____

282 _____ 35 _____

981 _____ 773 _____

On the lines below, explain how you decided whether to round each number up or down.

_____

_____

_____

_____

12 During the baseball season, Marvin's team won 5 games and lost 14 games.

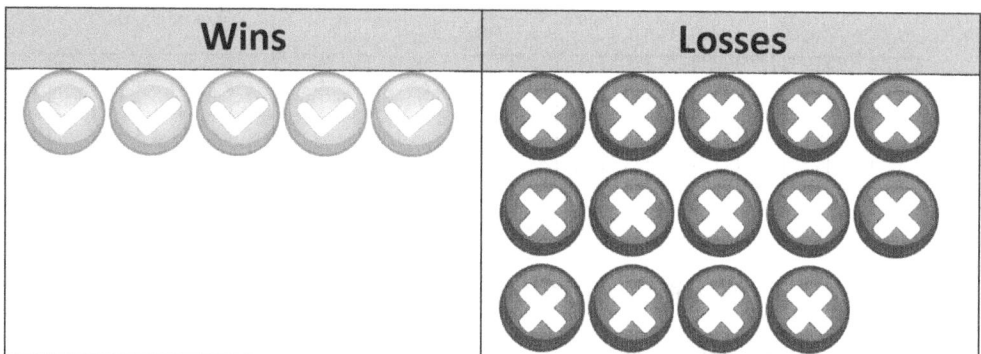

What fraction of the total games did the team win? Write your answer below.

_____

13 Shade the models below to show $\frac{3}{10}$ and $\frac{1}{5}$.

$\frac{3}{10}$ 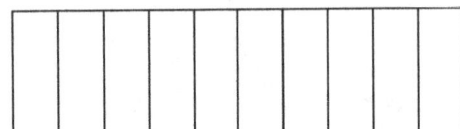 $\frac{1}{5}$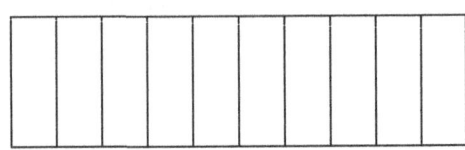

Place one of the symbols below in the number sentence to compare the fractions $\frac{3}{10}$ and $\frac{1}{5}$.

<, >, =

$\frac{3}{10}$ ☐ $\frac{1}{5}$

On the lines below, explain how the models helped you find the answer.

_____

_____

_____

14 Look at the pattern below.

16, 19, 22, 25, 28, 31, ____

Write an expression that can be used to find the next number in the pattern. Use *x* to represent the last number in the pattern.

Expression _____

Use the expression to find the next number in the pattern.

Answer _____

Use the expression to find the number that would come after 112.

Answer _____

15 Complete the number sentences below to show **three** different ways to complete the calculation in two steps.

$$6 \times 5 \times 3$$

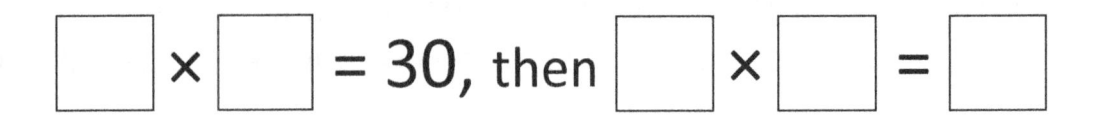

☐ × ☐ = 30, then ☐ × ☐ = ☐

☐ × ☐ = 18, then ☐ × ☐ = ☐

☐ × ☐ = 15, then ☐ × ☐ = ☐

16 A company has 8 salespersons. Each salesperson works about 40 hours each week. About how many hours do all the salespeople work in all?

Ⓐ 32

Ⓑ 48

Ⓒ 320

Ⓓ 480

17 A dance class usually has 30 students in it. On Monday, there were 6 students missing from the class and 2 extra students visiting the class. Write the correct symbols in the boxes to complete the number sentence that shows how many students were in the class on Monday. Then complete the calculation.

30 ☐ 6 ☐ 2 = ☐

18 There were 17,856 people living in Eastwood in 2009. What is the value of the digit 8 in 17,856?

- Ⓐ Eight hundred
- Ⓑ Eight thousand
- Ⓒ Eighty thousand
- Ⓓ Eighty

19 What fraction of the model is shaded?

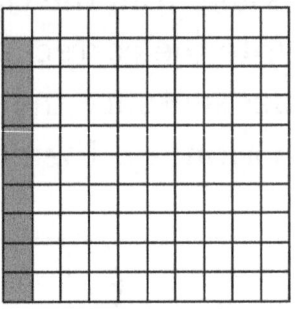

- Ⓐ $\frac{1}{9}$
- Ⓑ $\frac{9}{10}$
- Ⓒ $\frac{9}{91}$
- Ⓓ $\frac{9}{100}$

20 Which of the following is another way to write quarter past five?

- Ⓐ 5:25
- Ⓑ 5:30
- Ⓒ 5:45
- Ⓓ 5:15

END OF PRACTICE SET

SBAC Mathematics

Grade 3

Practice Set 4

Instructions

Read each question carefully. For each multiple-choice question, fill in the circle for the correct answer. For other types of questions, follow the directions given in the question.

You may use a ruler to help you answer questions. You may not use a calculator on this test.

This test should take 60 minutes to complete.

1   Which of these shows one way to divide a hexagon into two parts with equal areas?

Ⓐ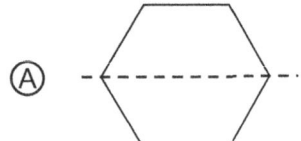

Ⓑ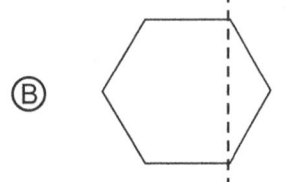

Ⓒ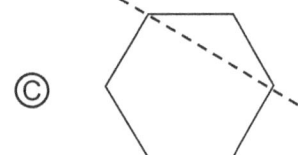

Ⓓ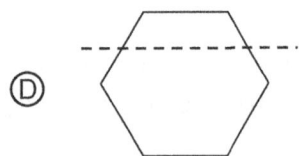

2   There were some people on a bus. After a stop, there were 4 times as many people on the bus. If there were 36 people on the bus after the stop, which equation can be used to find how many people, p, were on the bus to start with?

Ⓐ $p \times 4 = 36$

Ⓑ $p \div 4 = 36$

Ⓒ $p + 4 = 36$

Ⓓ $p - 4 = 36$

3 Inga made the design below.

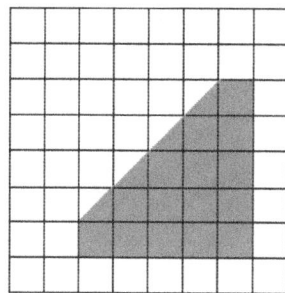

Each square measures 1 square centimeter. What is the area of the shaded part of the design?

- Ⓐ 16 square centimeters
- Ⓑ 17 square centimeters
- Ⓒ 18 square centimeters
- Ⓓ 19 square centimeters

4 Select **all** the statements that describe both a rectangle and a trapezoid.

- ☐ It has four sides.
- ☐ It is a quadrilateral.
- ☐ It has four equal angles.
- ☐ It is a parallelogram.
- ☐ It has two pairs of parallel sides.

5   What is the best estimate of the mass of a lemon?

- Ⓐ   2 grams
- Ⓑ   200 grams
- Ⓒ   2 kilograms
- Ⓓ   200 kilograms

6   Look at the number pattern below.

$$48, 42, 36, 30, 24, ...$$

If the pattern continues, what two numbers will come next?

- Ⓐ   22, 20
- Ⓑ   30, 36
- Ⓒ   20, 16
- Ⓓ   18, 12

7   Rita made the pictograph below to show how many cans each class collected for a food drive.

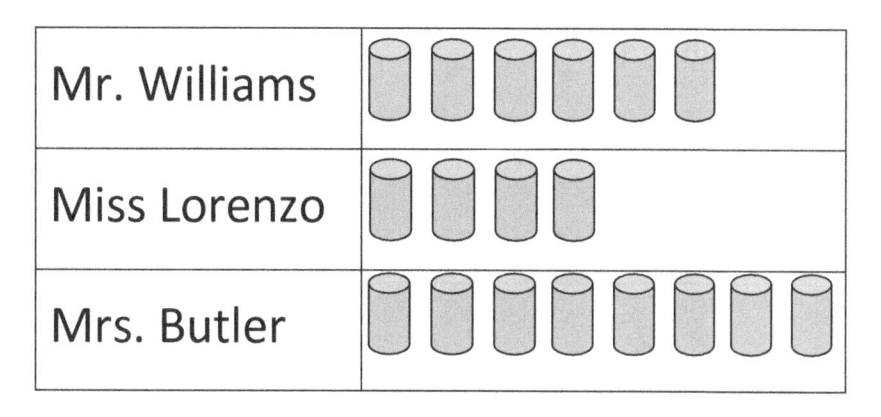

Mr. Williams	🥫🥫🥫🥫🥫
Miss Lorenzo	🥫🥫🥫
Mrs. Butler	🥫🥫🥫🥫🥫🥫🥫

🥫 = 4 cans

How many cans did Miss Lorenzo's class collect? Write your answer below.

_____ cans

8   What is the perimeter of the rectangle below?

3 cm

10 cm

Ⓐ   13 cm

Ⓑ   30 cm

Ⓒ   26 cm

Ⓓ   60 cm

37

9   Lei jogs for the same number of minutes every day. The table shows how far she jogs in total after 1, 2, 3, and 4 days. Complete the table to show how many minutes Lei jogs for in total after 5, 6, and 7 days.

Number of Days	Number of Minutes
1	15
2	30
3	45
4	60
5	
6	
7	

10   The table below shows how many coins of each type Joshua has.

Coin	Number of Coins
Penny	9
Nickel	4
Dime	5
Quarter	2

What fraction of the coins are quarters?

Ⓐ $\frac{1}{2}$

Ⓑ $\frac{1}{4}$

Ⓒ $\frac{1}{10}$

Ⓓ $\frac{1}{20}$

11 Round 8,782 to the nearest ten and the nearest hundred. Write your answers on the lines below.

Nearest ten _____

Nearest hundred _____

On the lines below, explain how you worked out whether to round the number up or down in each case.

_____

_____

_____

_____

12 Harris saved $96 in 16 weeks. He saved the same amount of money each week. How much did Harris save each week? Write your answer below.

$ _____

13 Joy got on a train at 1:35 p.m. Joy got off the train at 3:06 p.m. For how many minutes was Joy on the train? Write your answer below.

_____ minutes

14 Shade the fractions $\frac{1}{2}$ and $\frac{2}{4}$ on the fraction models below.

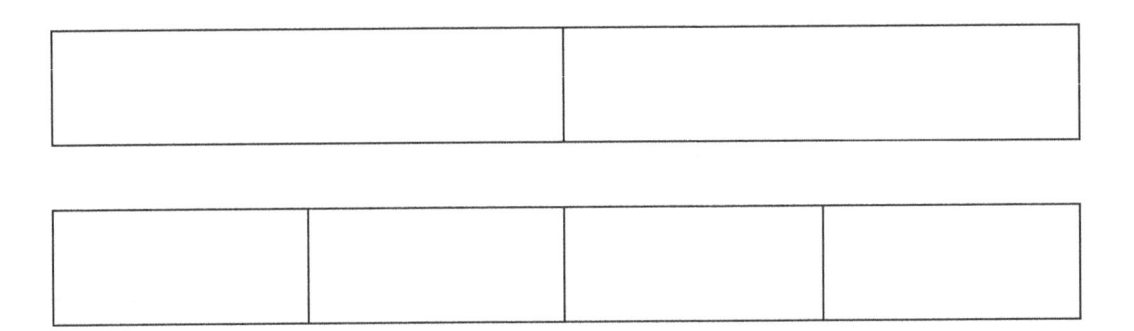

Shade the fraction model below to show another fraction equivalent to $\frac{1}{2}$ and $\frac{2}{4}$. Write the fraction on the line below.

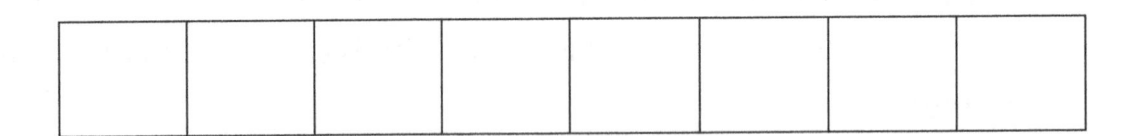

Fraction _____

15 What is the area of the rectangle shown on the grid below? Write your answer below.

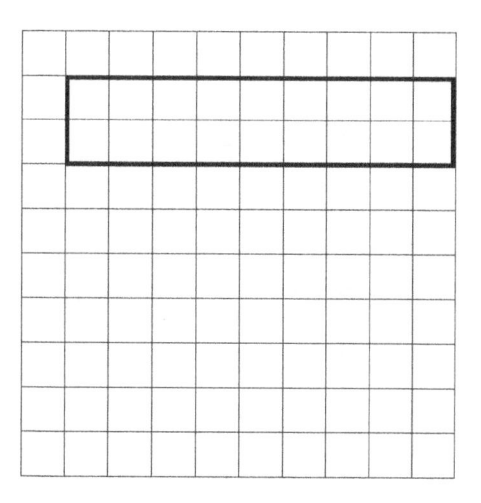

_____ square units

On the grid below, draw a rectangle with the same area but a different perimeter.

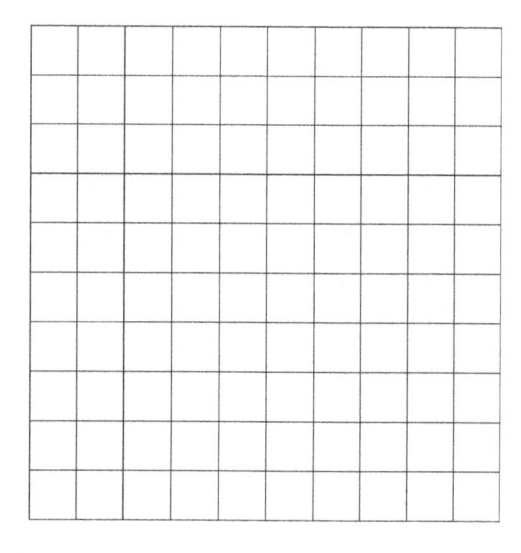

16 Margaret surveyed students about who they would vote for in a class election. Davis made the graph below to show the results.

Davis	☺☺☺☺
Bobby	
Inga	☺☺☺☺☺☺☺

Each ☺ means 2 students.

In the survey, 8 students said they would vote for Bobby. How many symbols should Margaret use to show 8 votes?

Ⓐ 8

Ⓑ 4

Ⓒ 2

Ⓓ 16

17 Kim is 63 inches tall. Chelsea is 4 inches taller than Kim. Vicky is 3 inches shorter than Chelsea. Which expression could be used to find Vicky's height, in inches?

Ⓐ 63 – 4 – 3

Ⓑ 63 + 4 + 3

Ⓒ 63 – 4 + 3

Ⓓ 63 + 4 – 3

18 Miss Jenkins received wages of $655. She saved $80 of her wages and spent the rest. How much money did Miss Jenkins spend? Write your answer below.

$ _____

19 Bananas sell for $3 per pound. Stacey buys 9 pounds of bananas. How much would the bananas cost?

- Ⓐ $12
- Ⓑ $27
- Ⓒ $18
- Ⓓ $21

20 A picture frame is 8 inches wide and 5 inches high. What is the perimeter of the frame?

- Ⓐ 26 inches
- Ⓑ 32 inches
- Ⓒ 20 inches
- Ⓓ 40 inches

END OF PRACTICE SET

SBAC Mathematics

Grade 3

Practice Set 5

Instructions

Read each question carefully. For each multiple-choice question, fill in the circle for the correct answer. For other types of questions, follow the directions given in the question.

You may use a ruler to help you answer questions. You may not use a calculator on this test.

This test should take 60 minutes to complete.

1   Sara walked around the four outside edges of a football field. If Sara recorded the total distance she walked, what would Sara have determined?

   Ⓐ   The area of the football field

   Ⓑ   The volume of the football field

   Ⓒ   The perimeter of the football field

   Ⓓ   The surface area of the football field

2   A piece of note paper has side lengths of 12 centimeters. What is the area of the piece of note paper?

   Ⓐ   48 square centimeters

   Ⓑ   72 square centimeters

   Ⓒ   120 square centimeters

   Ⓓ   144 square centimeters

3 Leah made 500 cakes of soap to sell at a fair. She sold 182 cakes of soap on Saturday. Then she sold 218 cakes of soap on Sunday. Choose the **two** expressions that can be used to find how many cakes of soap she had left.

☐ 500 + 182 + 218

☐ 500 + 182 – 218

☐ 500 – 182 – 218

☐ 500 – (182 + 218)

☐ 500 – (218 – 182)

☐ 500 + (218 – 182)

4 Michael drove 1,285 miles during a vacation. How far did Michael drive to the nearest hundred and the nearest ten? Write your answers below.

Nearest hundred: _____ miles

Nearest ten: _____ miles

5 Donna has 18 roses. She wants to put the roses into vases so that each vase has the same number of roses, with no roses left over.

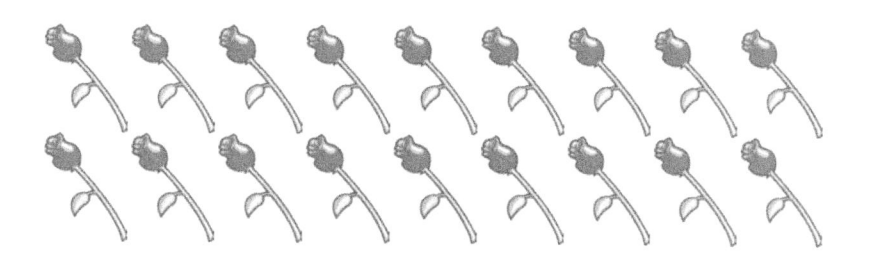

How many roses could Donna put in each vase?

Ⓐ 4
Ⓑ 5
Ⓒ 6
Ⓓ 8

6 Patrick bought 2 packets of 8 pencils for $4 per packet. He also bought 3 packets of 5 crayons for $3 per packet. How much did Patrick spend in all?

Ⓐ $17
Ⓑ $25
Ⓒ $47
Ⓓ $64

7 Look at the shaded figure below.

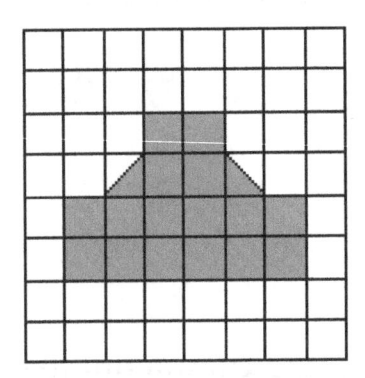

What is the area of the shaded figure?

Ⓐ 17 square units

Ⓑ 16 square units

Ⓒ 18 square units

Ⓓ 24 square units

8 Billy collects pennies and nickels. Billy has 142 pennies and 56 nickels in his coin collection. Which is the best estimate of the total number of coins in Billy's collection?

Ⓐ 150

Ⓑ 180

Ⓒ 200

Ⓓ 250

9   The figure below models the number sentence 6 × 2 = 12.

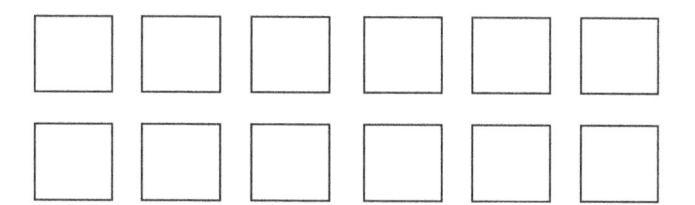

    Which number sentence is modeled by the same figure?

    Ⓐ   6 ÷ 2 = 3

    Ⓑ   36 ÷ 3 = 12

    Ⓒ   12 ÷ 6 = 2

    Ⓓ   24 ÷ 2 = 12

10 Which numbers make the number sentences below true? Write the numbers in the boxes.

    18 × ☐ = 18

    18 × ☐ = 0

11 The graph shows how far four students travel to school.

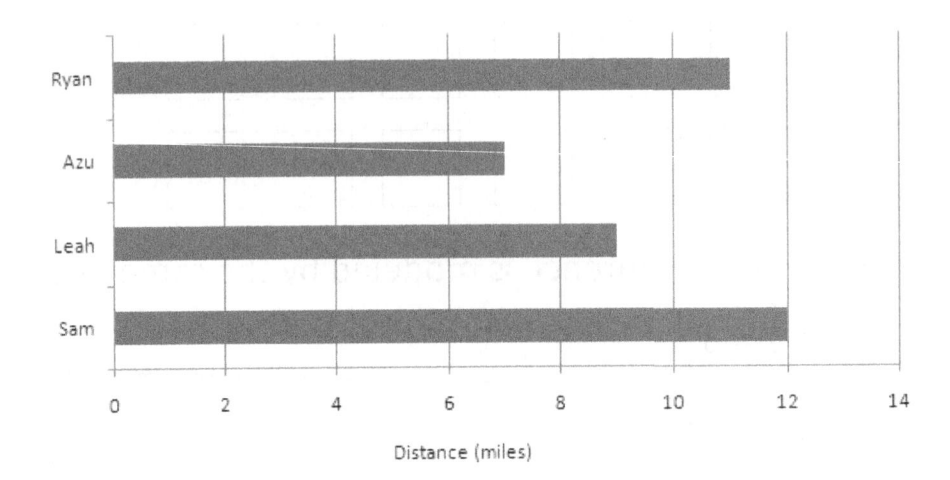

How much farther does Ryan travel than Azu? Write your answer below.

_____ miles

Which two students travel a total of 20 miles? Write your answer below.

_____ and _____

Claudia travels half the distance that Sam travels. How far does Claudia travel? Write your answer below.

_____ miles

12 What is the total area of the shaded portion of the grid?

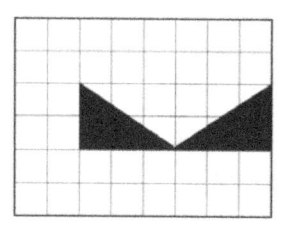

- Ⓐ 3 square units
- Ⓑ 6 square units
- Ⓒ 12 square units
- Ⓓ 16 square units

13 A school play was performed on three nights. The table below shows the number of people that saw the school play each night.

Day	Number of People
Friday	225
Saturday	318
Sunday	290

Which number sentence shows the best estimate of the total number of people who saw the school play?

- Ⓐ 200 + 300 + 200 = 700
- Ⓑ 200 + 300 + 300 = 800
- Ⓒ 200 + 400 + 300 = 900
- Ⓓ 300 + 400 + 300 = 1,000

14 Aaron has quarters and dimes. Aaron's coins are shown below.

Complete the **two** fractions that show the fraction of coins that are quarters.

$$\frac{\boxed{}}{6} = \frac{\boxed{}}{3}$$

15 Which number sentence represents the array shown below?

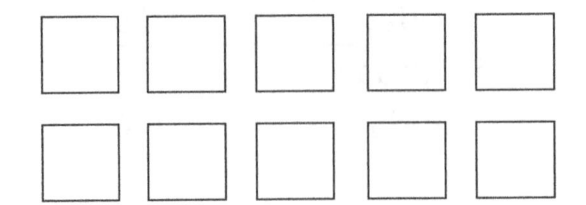

Ⓐ 5 + 2 = 7

Ⓑ 5 × 5 = 25

Ⓒ 5 × 2 = 10

Ⓓ 5 − 2 = 3

16 Plot the fraction $2\frac{3}{4}$ on the number line below.

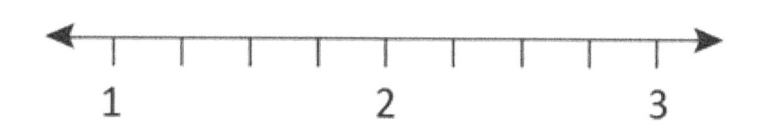

17 The table below shows the different colors of marbles in a bag.

Color	Number of Marbles
Red	5
Green	10
Blue	2
White	3

Match the color with what fraction of the marbles are that color. Draw lines to show the matches.

Red $\frac{1}{2}$

Green $\frac{1}{10}$

Blue $\frac{3}{20}$

White $\frac{1}{4}$

18 Leah baked 3 pies. She cut each pie into 8 pieces.

How many pieces of pie does Leah have? Write your answer below.

_____ pieces of pie

19 Sarah needs a screwdriver that is smaller than $\frac{3}{8}$ inch. Which screwdriver sizes are less than $\frac{3}{8}$ inch? Select **all** the correct answers.

☐ $\frac{1}{2}$ inch

☐ $\frac{3}{4}$ inch

☐ $\frac{1}{8}$ inch

☐ $\frac{1}{4}$ inch

☐ $\frac{3}{10}$ inch

☐ $\frac{5}{8}$ inch

20 A gift card has a length of 150 mm and a width of 50 mm. Complete the number sentences below to show **two** ways to find the perimeter of the gift card, in millimeters.

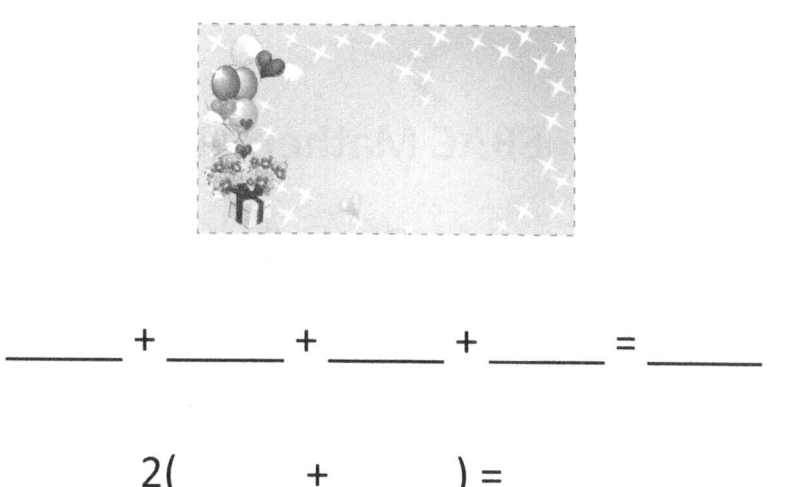

_____ + _____ + _____ + _____ = _____

2(_____ + _____) = _____

END OF PRACTICE SET

SBAC Mathematics

Grade 3

Practice Set 6

Instructions

Read each question carefully. For each multiple-choice question, fill in the circle for the correct answer. For other types of questions, follow the directions given in the question.

You may use a ruler to help you answer questions. You may not use a calculator on this test.

This test should take 60 minutes to complete.

1   Which of these shapes can be divided into two equal triangles by drawing a vertical line down the center?

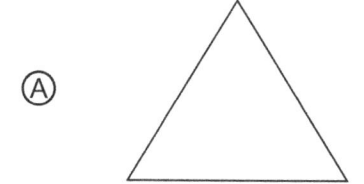

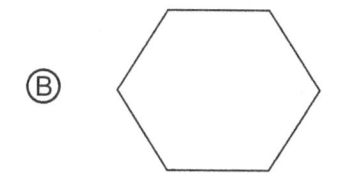

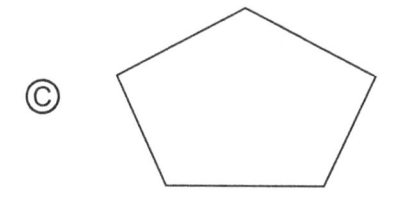

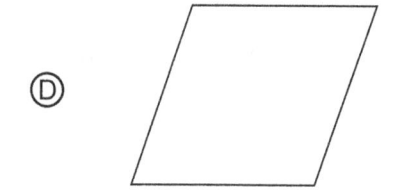

Ⓐ

Ⓑ

Ⓒ

Ⓓ

2 Kym is going camping. It costs $16 per night for the campsite. Kym plans to stay for 12 nights. How much will the campsite cost for 12 nights?

Ⓐ $82

Ⓑ $144

Ⓒ $168

Ⓓ $192

3 Andrew is selling muffins at a bake sale. The table shows the profit he makes by selling 5, 10, 15, and 20 muffins.

Muffins Sold	Profit Made
5	$15
10	$30
15	$45
20	$60

How much profit does Andrew make for selling 1 muffin? Write your answer below.

$_____

How many muffins will Andrew need to sell to make a profit of $150? Write your answer below.

_____ muffins

4 What is the area of the square below? Write your answer below.

6 cm

_____ cm²

5 Mrs. Bowen cooked dinner for 24 guests. She cooked 3 courses for each guest. Which equation shows how many courses Mrs. Bowen cooked, *c*?

- Ⓐ 24 × 3 = *c*
- Ⓑ 24 + 3 = *c*
- Ⓒ 24 − 3 = *c*
- Ⓓ 24 ÷ 3 = *c*

6 Which number is 3 more than the product of 4 and 23?

- Ⓐ 80
- Ⓑ 89
- Ⓒ 92
- Ⓓ 95

7 The graph below shows the high temperature in Dallas for five days.

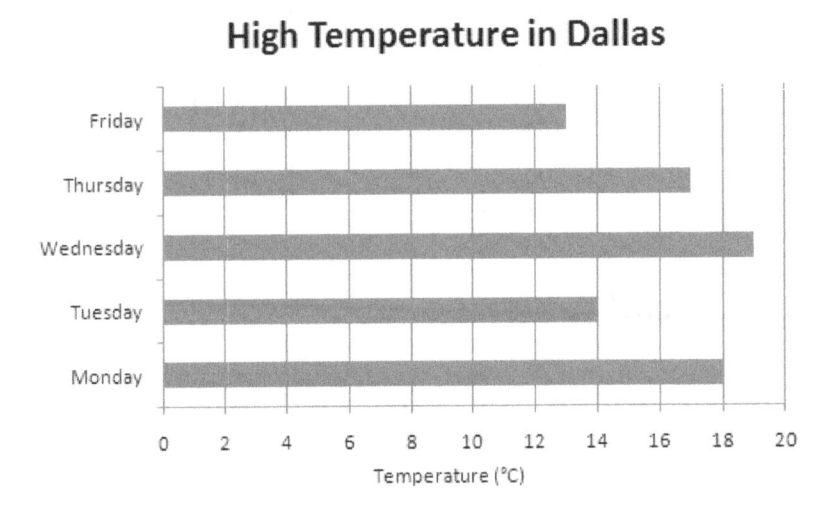

High Temperature in Dallas

Day	Temperature (°C)
Friday	13
Thursday	17
Wednesday	19
Tuesday	14
Monday	18

On which day was the high temperature 5°C less than the day with the highest temperature? Write your answer below.

_____

What was the high temperature on Friday? Write your answer below.

_____°

On Monday, the low temperature was half the high temperature. What was the low temperature on Monday? Write your answer below.

_____°

8 Shade the model below to show a fraction equivalent to $\frac{6}{8}$.

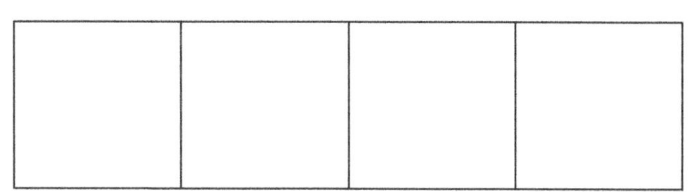

Write the fraction you shaded in lowest form. Write your answer below.

_____

9 Beads are sold in packets of 6 or packets of 8. Liz needs to buy exactly 30 beads. Which set of packets could Liz buy? Select **all** the correct answers.

☐   5 packets of 6 beads

☐   5 packets of 8 beads

☐   1 packet of 8 beads and 2 packets of 6 beads

☐   2 packets of 8 beads and 2 packets of 6 beads

☐   1 packet of 8 beads and 3 packets of 6 beads

☐   3 packets of 8 beads and 1 packet of 6 beads

10 Joy bought a pair of shorts for $11. Then she bought a scarf for $3. Joy had $18 left. Which equation could be used to find how much money Joy had to start with, *m*?

Ⓐ 18 − 11 + 3 = *m*

Ⓑ 18 + 11 − 3 = *m*

Ⓒ *m* + 11 + 3 = 18

Ⓓ *m* − 11 − 3 = 18

11 The graph shows how long Jody studied each week day.

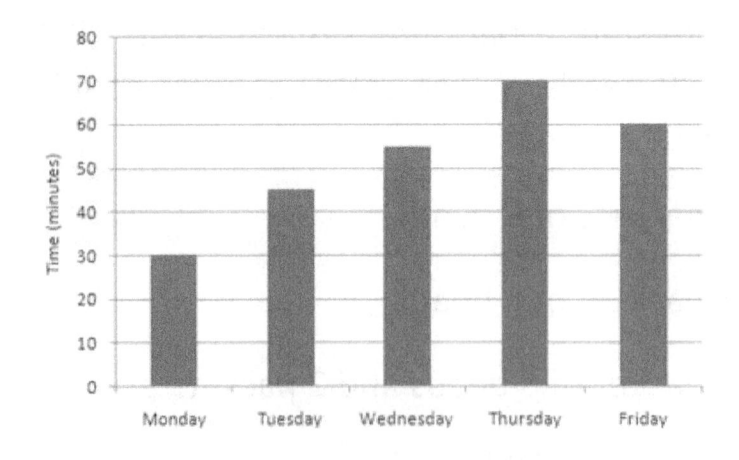

On which day did Jody study for 10 minutes more than the day before?

Ⓐ Tuesday

Ⓑ Wednesday

Ⓒ Thursday

Ⓓ Friday

12 Davis is making a pictograph to show how many letters three students wrote in a month.

Davis	✉✉✉
Bobby	
Inga	✉✉

Each ✉ means 2 letters.

Bobby wrote 8 letters. How many letter symbols should Davis use to show 8 letters?

Ⓐ 8

Ⓑ 4

Ⓒ 2

Ⓓ 16

13 Ray is slicing apples into 8 slices. Complete the table to show how many apple slices Ray will have if he uses 2, 4, and 5 apples.

Number of Apples	Number of Slices
2	
4	
5	

14 Look at the number pattern below. If the pattern continues, which **two** numbers will come next? Write your answers below.

$$4, 8, 12, 16, 20, \underline{}, \underline{}$$

15 Which fraction does the shaded model represent?

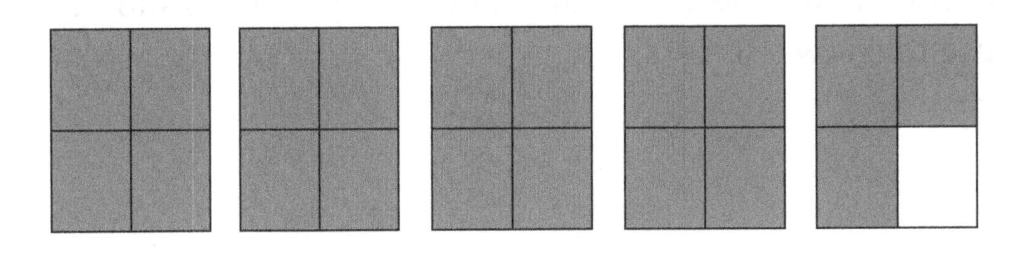

Ⓐ $4\frac{3}{4}$

Ⓑ $4\frac{1}{4}$

Ⓒ $5\frac{3}{4}$

Ⓓ $5\frac{1}{4}$

16 Which fraction model is equivalent to $\frac{1}{2}$?

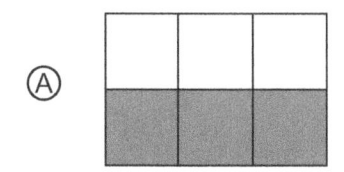

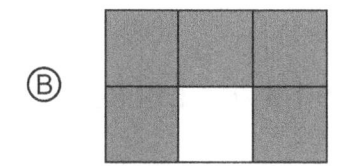

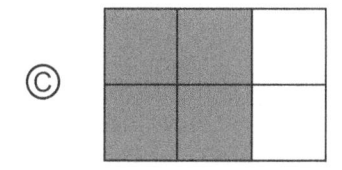

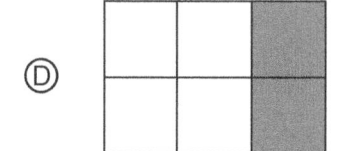

Ⓐ
Ⓑ
Ⓒ
Ⓓ

17 Damien folded the shirts and shorts shown below.

What fraction of the clothes folded were shorts? Write your answer below.

_____

18 David filled the bucket below with water.

About how much water would it take to fill the bucket?

Ⓐ 5 milliliters

Ⓑ 50 milliliters

Ⓒ 5 liters

Ⓓ 50 liters

19 The Walker family drove 182 miles on Saturday. Then they drove 218 miles on Sunday. How many miles did the family travel in all?

Ⓐ 300 miles

Ⓑ 290 miles

Ⓒ 400 miles

Ⓓ 390 miles

20 Margo sorts apples into 1 kilogram bags to sell. Which of these is most likely to be the number of apples in each bag?

- Ⓐ 2 apples
- Ⓑ 10 apples
- Ⓒ 50 apples
- Ⓓ 100 apples

END OF PRACTICE SET

SBAC Mathematics

Grade 3

Practice Set 7

Instructions

Read each question carefully. For each multiple-choice question, fill in the circle for the correct answer. For other types of questions, follow the directions given in the question.

You may use a ruler to help you answer questions. You may not use a calculator on this test.

This test should take 60 minutes to complete.

1 A bike ride was held to raise money. There were 70 riders and each rider paid $8 to enter. How much money was raised in all?

- Ⓐ $506
- Ⓑ $560
- Ⓒ $568
- Ⓓ $580

2 Sam read 39 pages of a novel in one week. He had 165 pages left to read. How many pages does the novel have? Write your answer below.

_____

3 If the numbers below are each rounded to the nearest hundred, which **two** numbers will be rounded up?

- ☐ 10,325
- ☐ 35,682
- ☐ 23,708
- ☐ 71,935
- ☐ 48,540
- ☐ 62,854

4 Leonie has 20 books. She placed an equal number of books on 5 different shelves. There were no books left over.

Which number sentence shows how many books Leonie put on each shelf?

- Ⓐ 20 + 5 = 25
- Ⓑ 20 − 5 = 15
- Ⓒ 20 × 5 = 100
- Ⓓ 20 ÷ 5 = 4

5 Shade the stars below so that $\frac{1}{3}$ of the stars are shaded.

6 A square garden has side lengths of 8 inches. What is the area of the garden?

- Ⓐ 32 square inches
- Ⓑ 36 square inches
- Ⓒ 48 square inches
- Ⓓ 64 square inches

7 Look at the shaded figure below.

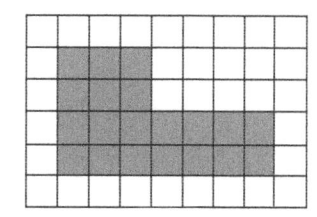

What is the area of the shaded figure?

- Ⓐ 20 square units
- Ⓑ 22 square units
- Ⓒ 26 square units
- Ⓓ 28 square units

8 Dannii is training for a bike race. She rode 17 miles on Monday, 19 miles on Tuesday, and 11 miles on Wednesday. Which is the best estimate of how far Dannii rode in all?

   Ⓐ 30 miles

   Ⓑ 40 miles

   Ⓒ 50 miles

   Ⓓ 60 miles

9 Squares and rectangles are quadrilaterals. Which of the shapes below is also a quadrilateral?

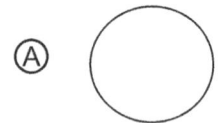

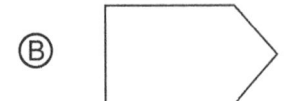

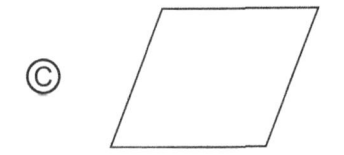

   Ⓐ

   Ⓑ

   Ⓒ

   Ⓓ

10   The triangle below has a perimeter of 26 cm.

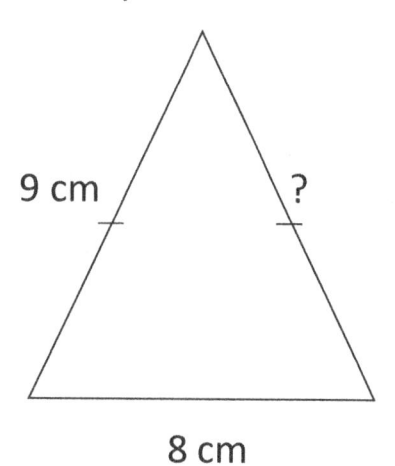

9 cm   ?

8 cm

What is the length of the missing side? Write your answer below.

_____ cm

11   One Friday, 5 of a hairdresser's customers were male and 15 were female. What fraction of the hairdresser's customers were male? Write your answer below in lowest form. You can use the diagram below to help find your answer.

_____ of the customers

12 Which number comes next in the pattern below? Write your answer on the line below.

4, 8, 16, 32, 64, ___

13 Alana finished school at the time shown on the clock below.

Alana arrived home 15 minutes later. What time did Alana arrive home? Write your answer below.

_____ p.m.

14 A box contains 60 cans of soup. Gerald orders 8 boxes of soup for his store. How many cans of soup does Gerald order? Write your answer below.

_____ cans of soup

15 Lyn lives 15 miles from her school. Dan lives 3 miles closer than Lyn. How far does Dan live from school? Write your answer below.

_____ miles

16 The graph shows the number of points four players scored in a basketball game.

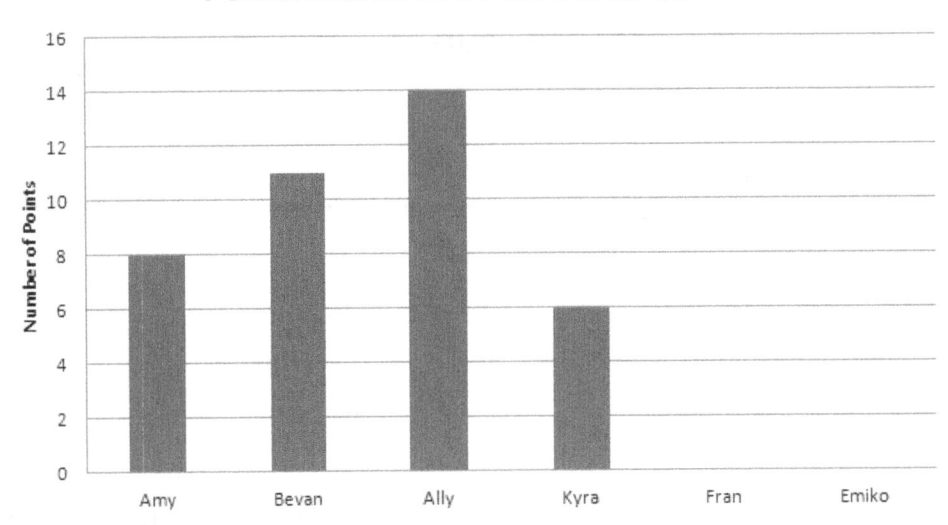

Points Scored in a Basketball Game

Fran scored 9 points and Emiko scored 5 points. Add two bars to the graph above to show the points scored by Fran and Emiko.

How many of the players scored more points than Fran? Write your answer below.

_____

17 Circle all the shapes below that are quadrilaterals.

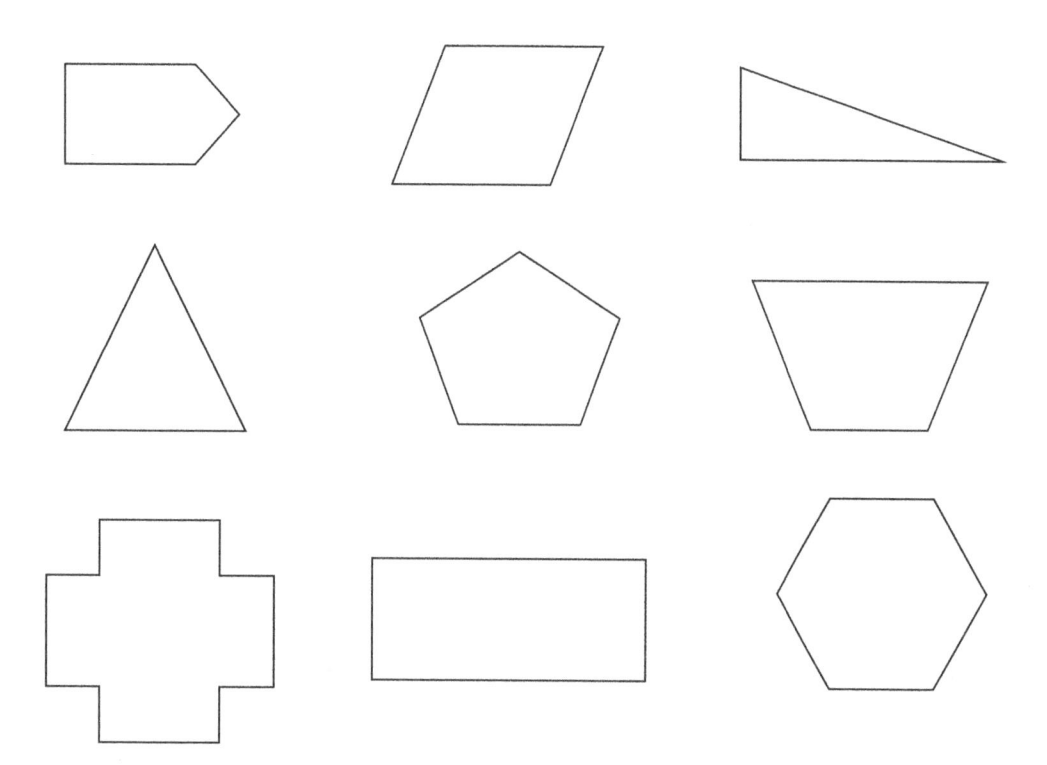

On the lines below, describe the property that is shared by all the shapes you circled.

_____

_____

_____

_____

18 Look at the figure below.

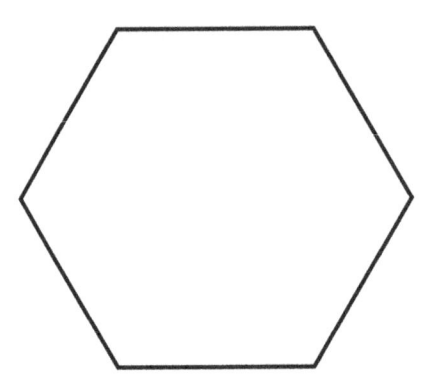

Divide the shape into 6 equal triangles. Draw lines on the shape above to show your answer.

Shade 2 of the triangles you divided the shape into. What fraction of the shape is shaded? Write your answer below.

_____

19 The top of a rectangular desk is 4 feet long and 3 feet wide. What is the area of the top of the desk? What is the perimeter of the top of the desk? Write your answers below.

Area: _____

Perimeter: _____

20 Look at the shapes below.

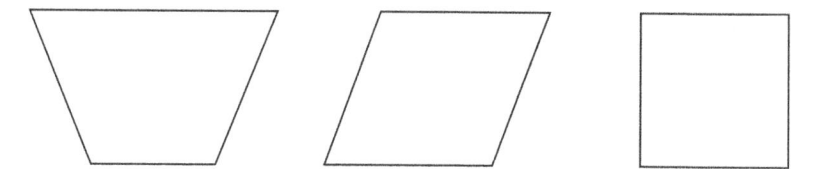

Circle the rhombus.

On the lines below, describe **two** ways a rhombus is similar to a square.

_____

_____

_____

_____

END OF PRACTICE SET

SBAC Mathematics

Grade 3

Practice Set 8

Instructions

Read each question carefully. For each multiple-choice question, fill in the circle for the correct answer. For other types of questions, follow the directions given in the question.

You may use a ruler to help you answer questions. You may not use a calculator on this test.

This test should take 60 minutes to complete.

1 What fraction of the letter cards below are vowels?

| A | E | T | P | S |

Ⓐ $\frac{1}{2}$

Ⓑ $\frac{2}{3}$

Ⓒ $\frac{1}{5}$

Ⓓ $\frac{2}{5}$

2 The graph below shows the number of pets four girls have.

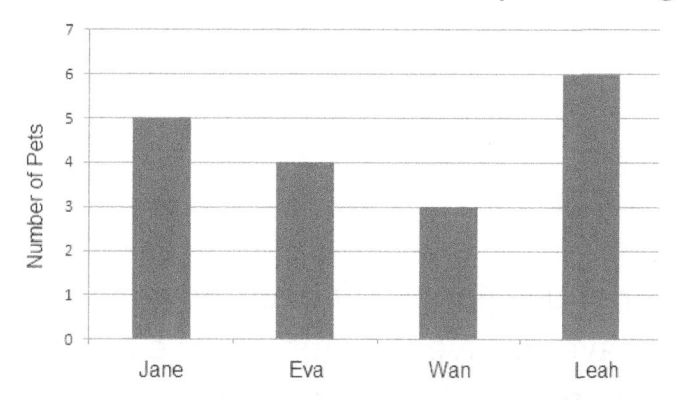

Which two girls have 10 pets in total? Write your answer below.

_____ and _____

3 Rory scored 28 points in a basketball game. Adam scored 4 points less than Rory. Danny scored 6 points more than Adam. How many points did Danny score?

Ⓐ 18

Ⓑ 30

Ⓒ 26

Ⓓ 38

4 Chan had a bag of 27 lollipops. He divided the lollipops evenly between several children.

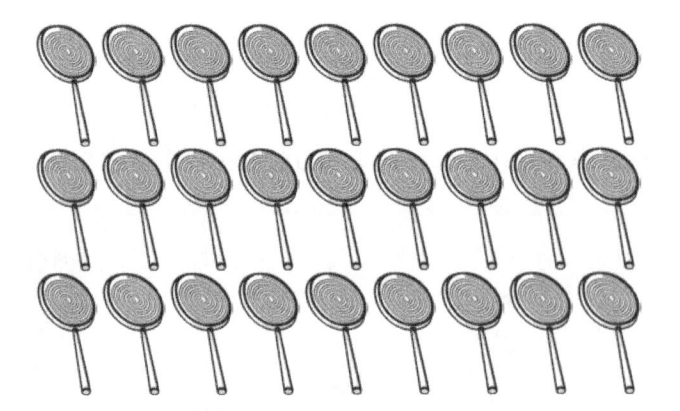

If there were no lollipops left over, how many lollipops could each child have received? Complete the number sentences below to find the **two** possible answers.

☐ ÷ ☐ = ☐

☐ ÷ ☐ = ☐

5 Each square on the grid below is 1 cm wide and 1 cm high.

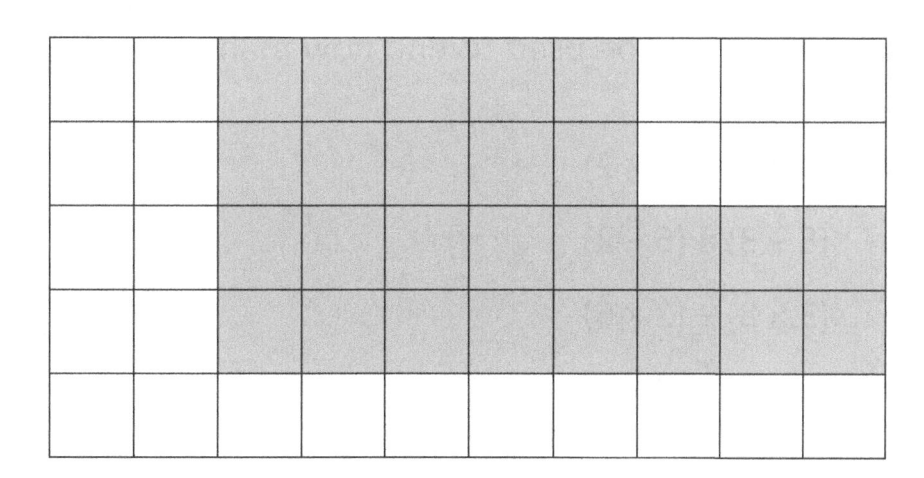

Which **two** expressions could be used to find the area of the shaded figure, in square centimeters?

- ☐ (5 x 4) + (3 x 2)

- ☐ (10 x 5) − (5 x 6)

- ☐ (8 x 2) + (5 x 4)

- ☐ (8 x 4) − (3 x 2)

- ☐ (8 x 4) − 3

- ☐ (10 x 5) − (2 x 6)

6 Ally bought 3 packets of pencils and 2 packets of pens. There were 8 pencils in each packet, and 6 pens in each packet. Which expression could be used to find how many more pencils she bought than pens?

- Ⓐ (8 × 6) − (3 × 2)
- Ⓑ (8 − 3) × (6 − 2)
- Ⓒ (3 × 8) − (2 × 6)
- Ⓓ (3 + 8) − (2 + 6)

7 Joy is making gift cards. She puts stars on the front of each card. The table shows how many stars she uses for 3, 5, and 6 cards.

Number of Cards	Number of Stars
3	12
5	20
6	24
8	

Based on the table, how many stars would Joy need to make 8 cards?

- Ⓐ 28
- Ⓑ 32
- Ⓒ 36
- Ⓓ 26

8 Ling scored 82 on a reading test. Mickey scored 63 on the reading test. Which is the best estimate of how many more points Ling scored than Mickey?

Ⓐ 10

Ⓑ 15

Ⓒ 20

Ⓓ 25

9 The graph below shows the number of different types of trees in an orchard.

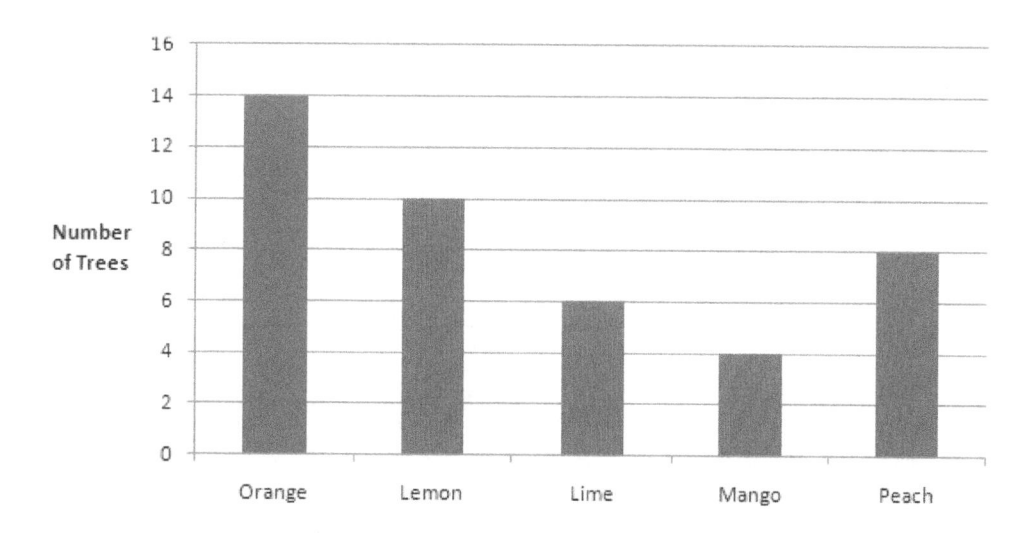

How many more orange trees are there than lime and mango trees combined? Write your answer below.

_____ trees

10 A diner has 18 tables. Each table can seat 4 people. The diner also has 8 benches that can each seat 6 people. How many people can the diner seat in all?

- Ⓐ 36
- Ⓑ 120
- Ⓒ 260
- Ⓓ 308

11 A rectangle has a length of 6 inches and a height of 5 inches. Complete the number sentences to show **two** ways to find the perimeter of the rectangle, in inches.

_____ + _____ + _____ + _____ = _____

2(_____ + _____) = _____

12 Gregory divided a rectangular piece of cardboard into sections, as shown below.

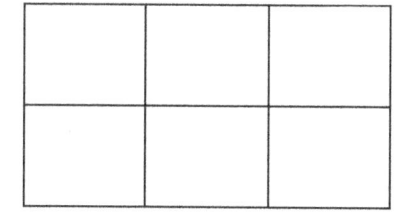

What fraction of the whole is each section?

Ⓐ $\frac{1}{2}$

Ⓑ $\frac{1}{3}$

Ⓒ $\frac{1}{5}$

Ⓓ $\frac{1}{6}$

13 What is the product of 9 and 8?

Ⓐ 56

Ⓑ 64

Ⓒ 72

Ⓓ 81

14. The grade 3 students at Sam's school are collecting cans for a food drive. The table below shows how many cans each class collected.

Class	Number of Cans
Miss Powell	39
Mr. Sato	22
Mrs. Joshi	26
Mr. Perez	37

Complete the list below by rounding each number to the nearest ten.

Miss Powell   40

Mr. Sato   _____

Mrs. Joshi   _____

Mr. Perez   _____

15 Janine bought a packet of muffins. The packet contained 2 chocolate muffins and 6 vanilla muffins.

Complete the **two** fractions that show the fraction of muffins that are chocolate.

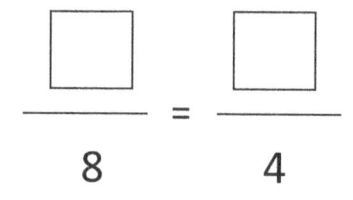

$$\frac{\Box}{8} = \frac{\Box}{4}$$

16 What fraction does point *J* represent?

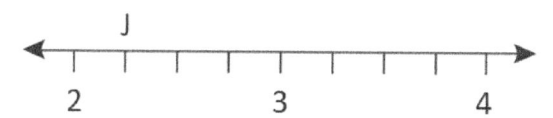

Ⓐ $2\frac{1}{4}$

Ⓑ $2\frac{1}{3}$

Ⓒ $2\frac{1}{5}$

Ⓓ $2\frac{1}{2}$

17 Which number sentence represents the array shown below?

Ⓐ 5 + 3 = 8

Ⓑ 5 × 3 = 15

Ⓒ 15 × 3 = 45

Ⓓ 20 − 5 = 15

18 A pizza has 8 slices. Eriko wants to order enough pizza to have at least 62 slices. What is the least number of pizzas Eriko could order? Write your answer below.

_____ pizzas

19   Tina completes the calculation below.

$$8 \times 5 = 40$$

Write a division equation that Tina could use to check her calculation.

☐ ÷ ☐ = ☐

20   What is the most likely mass of the pumpkin below?

- Ⓐ   5 grams
- Ⓑ   50 grams
- Ⓒ   5 kilograms
- Ⓓ   50 kilograms

END OF PRACTICE SET

SBAC Mathematics

Grade 3

Practice Set 9

Instructions

Read each question carefully. For each multiple-choice question, fill in the circle for the correct answer. For other types of questions, follow the directions given in the question.

You may use a ruler to help you answer questions. You may not use a calculator on this test.

This test should take 60 minutes to complete.

1. Habib measured the length of each wall of his room. A diagram of Habib's room is shown below.

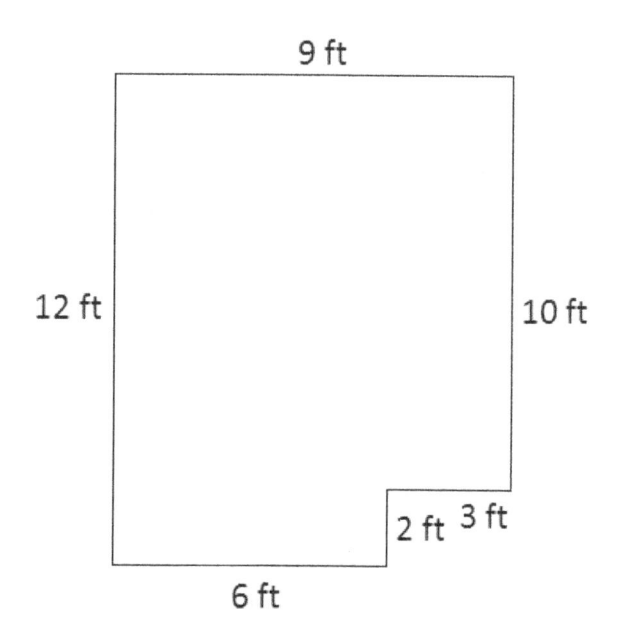

9 ft
12 ft
10 ft
2 ft 3 ft
6 ft

What is the perimeter of Habib's room?

Ⓐ 37 ft
Ⓑ 40 ft
Ⓒ 39 ft
Ⓓ 42 ft

2   Apples are sold in bags. There are the same number of apples in each bag. The table below shows the number of apples in 2, 3, and 4 bags. Complete the table to show the number of apples in 6 bags.

Number of Bags	Number of Apples
2	12
3	18
4	24
6	

3   Which shape below is a rectangle?

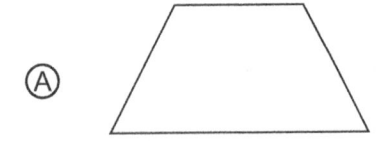

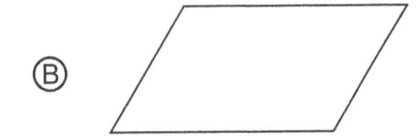

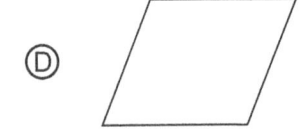

Ⓐ

Ⓑ

Ⓒ

Ⓓ

4 Toni has tokens for arcade games.

If Toni counts her tokens in groups of 6, which list shows only numbers she would count?

Ⓐ   6, 8, 10, 12

Ⓑ   6, 10, 16, 20

Ⓒ   12, 18, 24, 30

Ⓓ   12, 16, 20, 24

5 Which of these is another way of expressing 6 × 14?

Ⓐ   (6 × 10) + (6 × 4)

Ⓑ   (6 × 1) + (6 × 4)

Ⓒ   (6 × 10) + 4

Ⓓ   (6 × 4) + 10

6 There are 36 students in a class. The teacher needs to divide the students in the class into teams. Each team must have the same number of students in it. There cannot be any students left over. Which of the following could describe the teams? Select **all** the correct answers.

- [ ] 7 teams of 4 students
- [ ] 9 teams of 4 students
- [ ] 6 teams of 5 students
- [ ] 6 teams of 6 students
- [ ] 8 teams of 4 students
- [ ] 9 teams of 3 students

7 The pictograph shows the emails Sammy sent each week day.

Monday	✉✉✉
Tuesday	✉✉
Wednesday	✉✉✉✉
Thursday	✉✉
Friday	✉✉✉✉✉

Each ✉ means 2 emails.

How many emails did Sammy send on Wednesday? Write your answer below.

_____ emails

8 What time is shown on the clock below?

- Ⓐ 6:30
- Ⓑ 7:30
- Ⓒ 6:15
- Ⓓ 6:45

9 A square garden has side lengths of 8 inches. Jackie makes a rectangular garden with the same area as the square garden. Which of these could be the dimensions of the rectangular garden?

- Ⓐ 10 inches by 6 inches
- Ⓑ 7 inches by 9 inches
- Ⓒ 8 inches by 12 inches
- Ⓓ 16 inches by 4 inches

10 Naomi is making a pictograph to show how many fruit trees there are in her yard. The pictograph she has made so far is shown below.

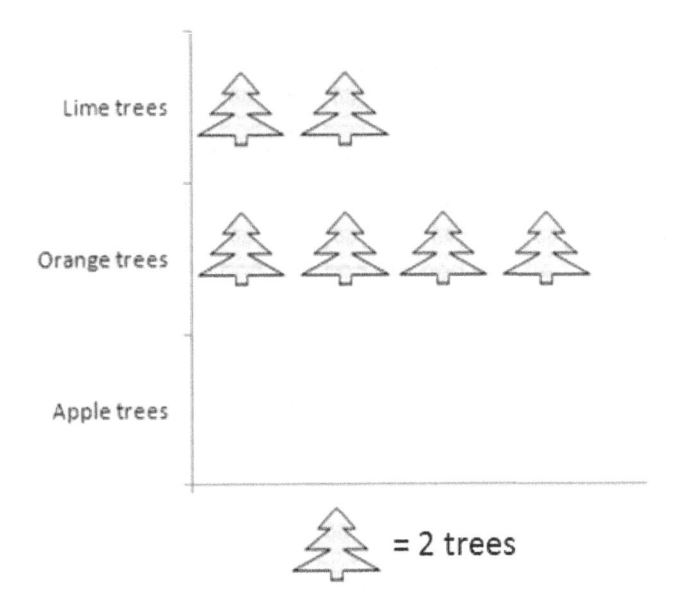

Lime trees	🌲 🌲
Orange trees	🌲 🌲 🌲 🌲
Apple trees	

🌲 = 2 trees

There are 6 apple trees in Naomi's yard. How many tree symbols should Naomi use to show 6 apple trees?

Ⓐ 3

Ⓑ 2

Ⓒ 12

Ⓓ 6

11 Chloe has a 2,000 gram bag of flour. She divides it into smaller bags of 250 grams each. How many smaller bags does she divide the flour into?

Ⓐ 4
Ⓑ 5
Ⓒ 8
Ⓓ 10

12 Shade the model below to show a fraction equivalent to $\frac{1}{4}$.

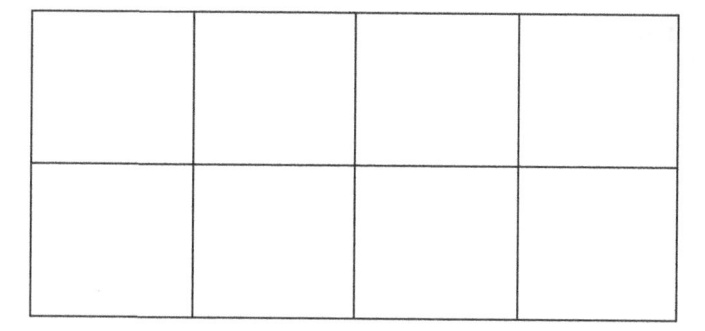

13 A school has 7 school buses. Each bus can seat 48 students. What is the total number of students the buses can seat? Write your answer below.

_____ students

14 What is the length of the piece of lace shown below?

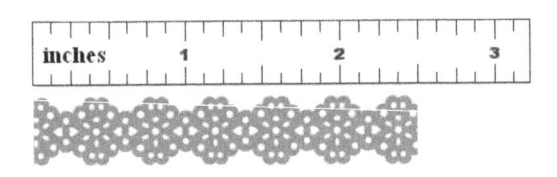

Ⓐ 2 inches

Ⓑ $2\frac{1}{2}$ inches

Ⓒ $2\frac{1}{3}$ inches

Ⓓ $2\frac{1}{4}$ inches

15 Ribbon costs $4 per yard. Allie has $24 to spend on ribbon. Which equation could be used to find how many yards of ribbon, y, she can buy?

Ⓐ 4 × 24 = y

Ⓑ 4 ÷ 24 = y

Ⓒ 4 × y = 24

Ⓓ 4 ÷ y = 24

16 Reggie's train leaves at the time shown on the clock below.

What time does Reggie's train leave?

Ⓐ   3:00

Ⓑ   1:15

Ⓒ   1:10

Ⓓ   3:05

17 What do the shaded models below show?

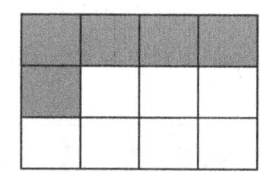

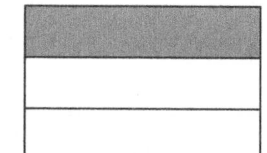

Ⓐ $\frac{5}{12} > \frac{1}{3}$

Ⓑ $\frac{5}{12} = \frac{1}{3}$

Ⓒ $\frac{5}{12} < \frac{4}{12}$

Ⓓ $\frac{5}{7} < \frac{2}{3}$

18 Which number sentence represents the array shown below?

Ⓐ 5 + 4 = 9

Ⓑ 5 × 5 = 25

Ⓒ 5 × 4 = 20

Ⓓ 5 – 4 = 1

19 Lydia eats 2 pieces of fruit every day. Complete the table to show how many pieces of fruit Lydia eats in 5, 7, and 14 days.

Number of Days	Number of Pieces of Fruit
5	
7	
14	

20 Melinda buys bagels in packets of 4.

If Melinda counts the bagels in groups of 4, which numbers would she count? Circle **all** the numbers she would count.

18	20	22	26
30	32	42	44

END OF PRACTICE SET

SBAC Mathematics

Grade 3

Practice Set 10

Instructions

Read each question carefully. For each multiple-choice question, fill in the circle for the correct answer. For other types of questions, follow the directions given in the question.

You may use a ruler to help you answer questions. You may not use a calculator on this test.

This test should take 60 minutes to complete.

1   Tim scored 21 points in a basketball game. Emmett scored 7 more points than Tim. Which method can be used to find how many points Tim and Emmett scored together?

   Ⓐ   Add 21 and 7

   Ⓑ   Add 21 to the sum of 21 and 7

   Ⓒ   Add 21 to the difference of 21 and 7

   Ⓓ   Subtract 7 from 21

2   Place the fractions below in order from smallest to greatest. Write the numbers 1, 2, 3, and 4 on the lines to show the order.

   ___ $\frac{7}{10}$

   ___ $\frac{4}{5}$

   ___ $\frac{1}{5}$

   ___ $\frac{9}{10}$

3   There are 28 students at basketball training. The coach needs to divide the students into groups. Each group must have the same number of students in it. There cannot be any students left over. Which of the following could describe the groups?

   Ⓐ   7 groups of 4 students

   Ⓑ   8 groups of 3 students

   Ⓒ   6 groups of 4 students

   Ⓓ   10 groups of 3 students

4   Annie collects baseball cards. She has 22 cards in her collection. She gave her sister 2 baseball cards. Then Annie bought 4 new baseball cards. Which expression can be used to find the number of baseball cards Annie has now?

   Ⓐ   22 + 2 + 4

   Ⓑ   22 + 2 − 4

   Ⓒ   22 − 2 + 4

   Ⓓ   22 − 2 − 4

5   Nate plotted a fraction on the number line below.

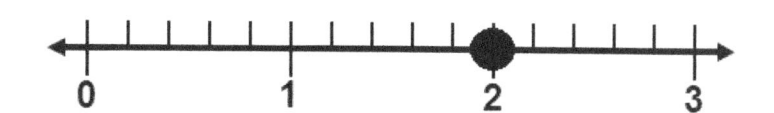

Which fractions could Nate have been plotting? Select **all** the correct answers.

☐ $\frac{1}{2}$

☐ $\frac{2}{2}$

☐ $\frac{4}{2}$

☐ $\frac{8}{4}$

☐ $\frac{4}{8}$

6   The pictograph below shows how long Tamika spent at the computer each week day.

Monday	🖥🖥🖥🖥
Tuesday	🖥🖥🖥🖥🖥🖥
Wednesday	🖥🖥🖥🖥🖥
Thursday	🖥🖥🖥
Friday	🖥🖥

Each 🖥 means 10 minutes.

How long did Tamika spend at the computer on Wednesday?

Ⓐ   15 minutes

Ⓑ   60 minutes

Ⓒ   5 minutes

Ⓓ   50 minutes

7   A recipe for meatballs calls for $\frac{1}{2}$ teaspoon of cumin. Complete the fractions below to show **two** fractions equivalent to $\frac{1}{2}$.

$$\frac{\Box}{6} \text{ and } \frac{6}{\Box}$$

8 Dean drew these shapes.

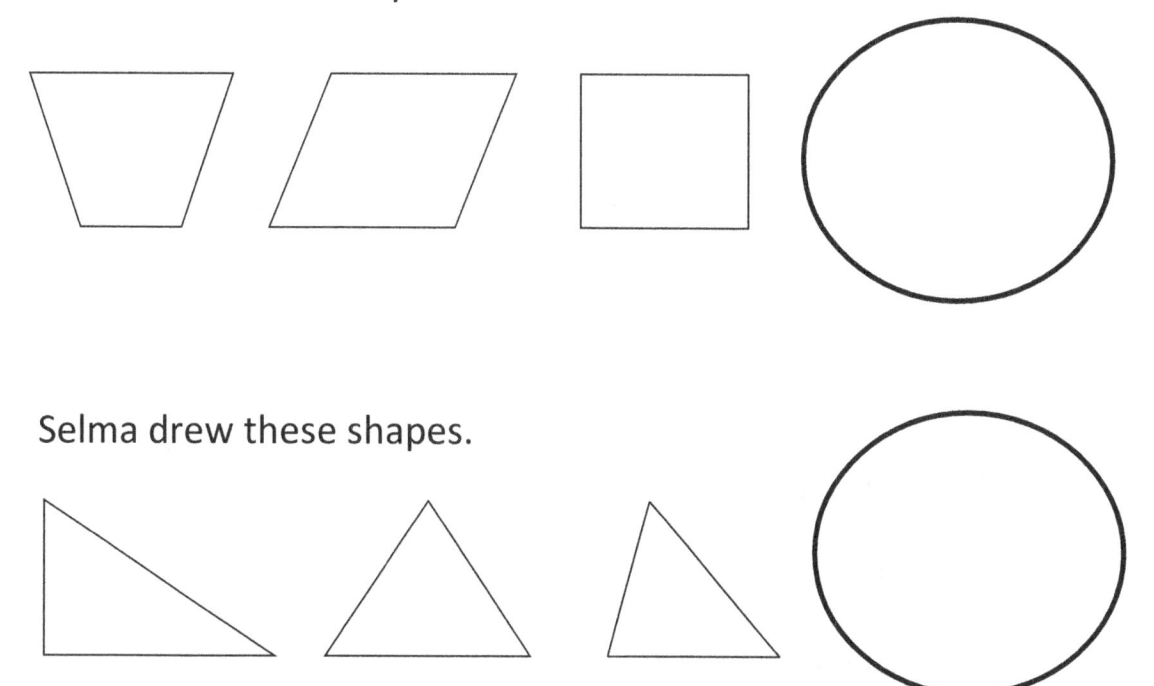

Selma drew these shapes.

Add **one** of the shapes below to Dean's shapes and **one** of the shapes below to Selma's shapes. Draw each shape in the empty circle.

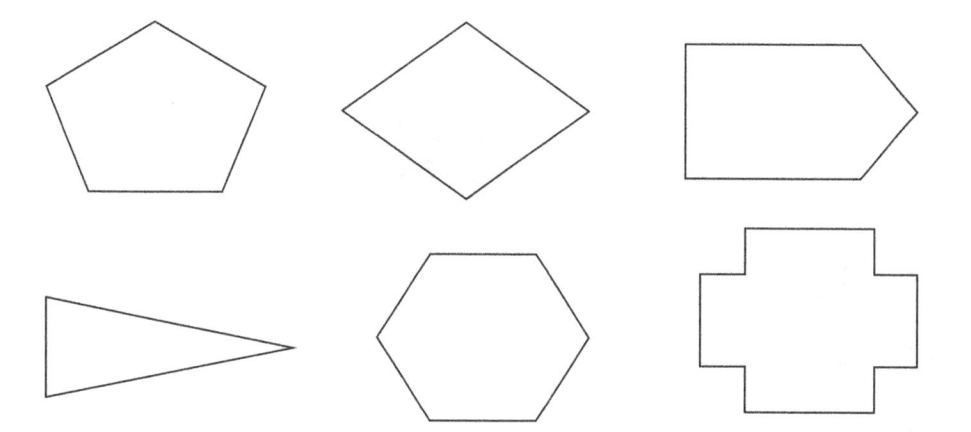

9 A piece of square note paper has side lengths of 5 inches each. What is the perimeter of the note paper?

- Ⓐ 10 inches
- Ⓑ 20 inches
- Ⓒ 25 inches
- Ⓓ 30 inches

10 Which measurement is the most likely mass of the apple?

- Ⓐ 1 gram
- Ⓑ 10 grams
- Ⓒ 100 grams
- Ⓓ 1,000 grams

11 Plot the number 48 on the number line below.

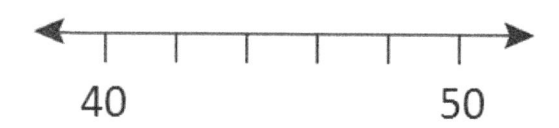

```
◄—┬—┬—┬—┬—┬—┬—┬—►
   40          50
```

What is the number 48 rounded to the nearest ten? Write your answer below.

_____

On the lines below, explain how the number line helped you round the number.

_____

_____

_____

_____

_____

12 Apple trees were planted in rows. Each row had the same number of apple trees. Complete the missing numbers in the table below.

Number of Rows	Number of Apple Trees
4	24
5	30
6	36
7	42
8	
9	
10	

13 Mrs. Anderson took out a loan that will take her 60 months to pay off. How many years will it take Mrs. Anderson to pay off the loan? Write your answer below.

1 year = 12 months

_____ years

14 Georgia shaded the shape below.

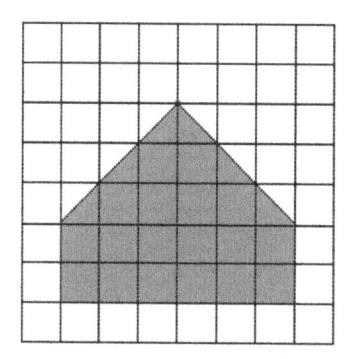

Each square on the grid measures 1 square centimeter. What is the area of the shaded shape? Write your answer below.

_____ square centimeters

15 The table below shows how many customers a restaurant had on each day of the week.

Day	Number of Customers
Monday	28
Tuesday	21
Wednesday	36
Thursday	32
Friday	45

How many more customers did the restaurant have on Friday than on Monday? Write your answer below.

_____ customers

16 The table below shows Emma's savings over four months.

Month	Amount Saved ($)
Jan	18
Feb	16
Mar	14
Apr	19

Complete the graph below using the data in the table.

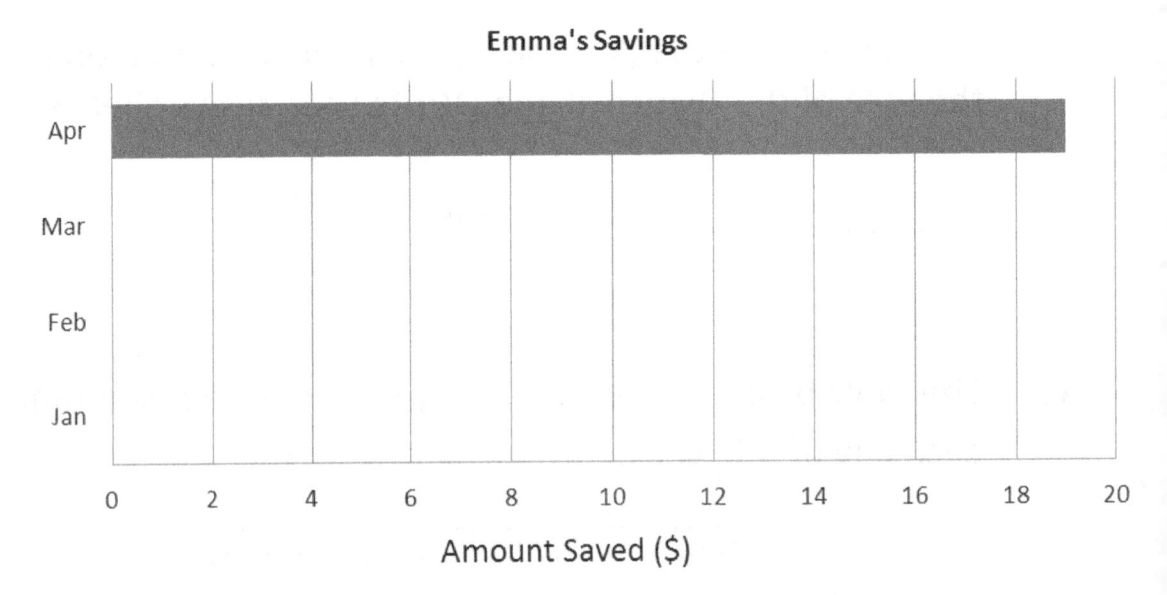

Emma's Savings

What is the difference between the most and the least she saved each month? Write your answer below.

$ _____

17 Look at the number pattern below.

$$7, 10, 13, 16, 19, 22, \underline{\quad}$$

If the pattern continues, which number will come next? Write your answer below.

_____

On the lines below, explain how you found your answer.

_____

_____

_____

_____

18 The picture below represents a playground.

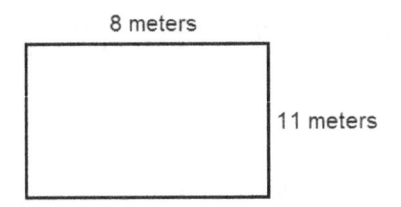

```
        8 meters
    ┌─────────────┐
    │             │ 11 meters
    │             │
    └─────────────┘
```

A fence is being built to go around the edge of the playground. The timber for the fence costs $14 per meter. If enough timber is bought to fit exactly around the edge of the playground, how much will the timber cost? Write your answer below.

$_____

19 During a golf game, Gia scored below par on 3 of the 18 holes.

Divide the rectangle below into segments and shade the rectangle to show what fraction of the holes Gia scored below par on.

What fraction of the holes did Gia score below par on? Write your answer below in lowest form.

_____

20 What are the two smallest 3-digit numbers that can be made using the digits 1, 6, and 4? Each digit must be used only once in each number. Write the two numbers below.

_____ and _____

On the lines below, explain how you found your answer.

_____

_____

_____

_____

END OF PRACTICE SET

ANSWER KEY

Common Core State Standards

The state of California has adopted the Common Core State Standards. These standards describe what students are expected to know. Student learning throughout the year is based on these standards, and all the questions on the Smarter Balanced assessments cover these standards. All the exercises and questions in this book cover the Common Core State Standards.

Assessing Skills and Knowledge

The skills listed in the Common Core State Standards are divided into five topics, or clusters. These are:

- Operations and Algebraic Thinking
- Number and Operations in Base Ten
- Number and Operations – Fractions
- Measurement and Data
- Geometry

The answer key identifies the topic for each question. Use the topics listed to identify general areas of strength and weakness. Then target revision and instruction accordingly.

The answer key also identifies the specific math skill that each question is testing. Use the skills listed to identify skills that the student is lacking. Then target revision and instruction accordingly.

Scoring Questions

This book includes questions where a task needs to be completed or a written answer is provided. The answer key gives guidance on what to look for in the answer and how to score these questions. Use the criteria listed as a guide to scoring these questions, and as a guide for giving the student advice on how to improve an answer.

SBAC Mathematics, Practice Set 1

Question	Answer	Topic	Common Core State Standard
1	B	Number & Operations-Fractions	Understand a fraction as a number on the number line; represent fractions on a number line diagram.
2	B	Measurement & Data	Tell and write time to the nearest minute and measure time intervals in minutes. Solve word problems involving addition and subtraction of time intervals in minutes.
3	A	Measurement & Data	Measure and estimate liquid volumes and masses of objects using standard units of grams (g), kilograms (kg), and liters (l).
4	(4 × 8) + 5 37	Operations/Algebraic Thinking	Solve two-step word problems using the four operations. Represent these problems using equations with a letter standing for the unknown quantity.
5	1st, 3rd, 5th, and 6th	Operations/Algebraic Thinking	Fluently multiply and divide within 100, using strategies such as the relationship between multiplication and division or properties of operations.
6	See Below	Number & Operations-Fractions	Understand a fraction as a number on the number line; represent fractions on a number line diagram. Express whole numbers as fractions, and recognize fractions that are equivalent to whole numbers.
7	See Below	Measurement & Data	Draw a scaled bar graph to represent a data set with several categories.
8	See Below	Geometry	Understand that shapes in different categories (e.g., rhombuses, rectangles, and others) may share attributes (e.g., having four sides), and that the shared attributes can define a larger category (e.g., quadrilaterals).
9	See Below	Measurement & Data	Find areas of rectilinear figures by decomposing them into non-overlapping rectangles and adding the areas of the non-overlapping parts. Solve real world and mathematical problems involving perimeters of polygons, including finding the perimeter given the side lengths.
10	See Below	Measurement & Data	Solve mathematical problems involving perimeters of polygons, including exhibiting rectangles with the same perimeter and different areas or with the same area and different perimeters.

Q6.
The numbers should be plotted as below.

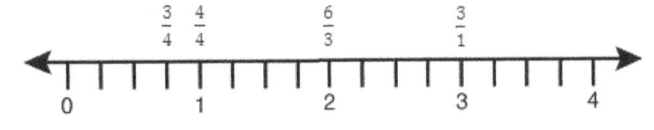

$\frac{3}{4}$ and $\frac{4}{4}$ between 0 and 1; $\frac{6}{3}$ at 2; $\frac{3}{1}$ at 3 on a number line from 0 to 4.

Scoring Information
Give a total score out of 2.
Give a score of 0.5 for each number correctly plotted.

Q7.
The graph should be completed with a bar to 12 for Action, a bar to 14 for Comedy, and a bar to 8 for Drama.

Scoring Information
Give a total score out of 3.
Give a score of 1 for each bar correctly added.

Q8.
The student should circle the trapezoid.
The student should explain that the trapezoid does not have two pairs of parallel sides or that the trapezoid only has one pair of parallel sides. The answer should show an understanding that parallelograms have two pairs of parallel sides.

Scoring Information
Give a total score out of 3.
Give a score of 1 for circling the trapezoid.
Give a score out of 2 for the explanation.

Q9.
The student should complete the missing dimensions of 2 ft and 11 ft.
The student may divide the shape into a 3 by 7 rectangle and a 2 by 8 rectangle or a 3 by 5 rectangle and an 11 by 2 rectangle.
The student should find an area of 37 square feet.
The student should find a perimeter of 36 feet.

Scoring Information
Give a total score out of 4.
Give a score of 0.5 for each correct missing dimension.
Give a score of 1 for dividing the shape correctly.
Give a score of 1 for the correct area.
Give a score of 1 for the correct perimeter.

Q10.
The student should draw a 6 by 2 rectangle on the grid.
The student should explain that the second rectangle has an area of 12 square units, but a perimeter of 14 units. The answer should show an understanding that rectangles with the same area do not always have the same perimeter.

Scoring Information
Give a total score out of 3.
Give a score of 1 for drawing a correct rectangle.
Give a score out of 2 for the explanation.

SBAC Mathematics, Practice Set 2

Question	Answer	Topic	Common Core State Standard
1	C	Number & Operations in Base Ten	Fluently add and subtract within 1000 using strategies and algorithms.
2	5, 10, 15, 20, 25	Operations/Algebraic Thinking	Identify arithmetic patterns, and explain them using properties of operations.
3	B	Measurement & Data	Tell and write time to the nearest minute and measure time intervals in minutes.
4	$1\frac{1}{4}$ inches or 1.25 inches	Measurement & Data	Generate measurement data by measuring lengths using rulers marked with halves and fourths of an inch.
5	2nd, 3rd, and 4th	Number & Operations-Fractions	Recognize and generate simple equivalent fractions. Explain why the fractions are equivalent, e.g., by using a visual fraction model.
6	C	Operations/Algebraic Thinking	Use multiplication and division within 100 to solve word problems in situations involving equal groups, arrays, and measurement quantities.
7	$717	Number & Operations in Base Ten	Fluently add and subtract within 1000 using strategies and algorithms.
8	See Below	Operations/Algebraic Thinking	Identify arithmetic patterns, and explain them using properties of operations.
9	See Below	Measurement & Data	Draw a scaled bar graph to represent a data set with several categories. Solve one- and two-step "how many more" and "how many less" problems using information presented in scaled bar graphs.
10	See Below	Measurement & Data	Find areas of rectilinear figures by decomposing them into non-overlapping rectangles and adding the areas of the non-overlapping parts.

Q8.
26, 30, 34, 38
The student should identify that all the numbers will be even. The student should explain that all the numbers will be even because an even number is always being added to an even number.

Scoring Information
Give a total score out of 4.
Give a score of 0.5 for each correct number in the pattern.
Give a score of 1 for identifying that all the numbers will be even and a score out of 1 for the explanation.

Q9.
Friday
40 minutes
30 minutes

Scoring Information
Give a total score out of 3.
Give a score of 1 for each correct answer.

Q10.
Rectangle 1: 2 by 4 units   Rectangle 2: 2 by 6 units
Area: 20 square units

Scoring Information
Give a total score out of 3.
Give a score of 1 for each correct answer.

SBAC Mathematics, Practice Set 3

Question	Answer	Topic	Common Core State Standard
1	18, 30, 36, 42	Operations/Algebraic Thinking	Interpret products of whole numbers, e.g., interpret 5 × 7 as the total number of objects in 5 groups of 7 objects each.
2	Wednesday	Measurement & Data	Solve one- and two-step "how many more" and "how many less" problems using information presented in scaled bar graphs.
3	$\frac{4}{1}$ and $\frac{12}{3}$	Number & Operations-Fractions	Express whole numbers as fractions, and recognize fractions that are equivalent to whole numbers.
4	B	Measurement & Data	Draw a scaled picture graph to represent a data set with several categories.
5	B	Operations/Algebraic Thinking	Solve two-step word problems using the four operations.
6	C	Operations/Algebraic Thinking	Represent problems using equations with a letter standing for the unknown quantity.
7	25,600	Number & Operations in Base Ten	Use place value understanding to round whole numbers to the nearest 10 or 100.
8	1,500 + 1,600 + 1,200 = 4,300	Operations/Algebraic Thinking	Assess the reasonableness of answers using mental computation and estimation strategies including rounding.
9	A	Number & Operations in Base Ten	Fluently add and subtract within 1000 using strategies and algorithms based on place value, properties of operations, and/or the relationship between addition and subtraction.
10	Point at $1\frac{1}{4}$	Number & Operations-Fractions	Understand a fraction as a number on the number line; represent fractions on a number line diagram.
11	See Below	Number & Operations in Base Ten	Use place value understanding to round whole numbers to the nearest 10 or 100.
12	$\frac{5}{19}$	Number & Operations-Fractions	Understand a fraction 1/b as the quantity formed by 1 part when a whole is partitioned into b equal parts.
13	See Below	Number & Operations-Fractions	Compare two fractions with the same numerator or the same denominator by reasoning about their size. Record the results of comparisons with the symbols >, =, or <, and justify the conclusions, e.g., by using a visual fraction model.
14	See Below	Operations/Algebraic Thinking	Identify arithmetic patterns, and explain them using properties of operations.
15	See Below	Operations/Algebraic Thinking	Apply properties of operations as strategies to multiply and divide.
16	C	Number & Operations in Base Ten	Multiply one-digit whole numbers by multiples of 10 in the range 10–90 using strategies based on place value and properties of operations.
17	30 – 6 + 2 = 26	Operations/Algebraic Thinking	Solve two-step word problems using the four operations. Represent these problems using equations with a letter standing for the unknown quantity.
18	A	Number & Operations in Base Ten	Use place value understanding.
19	D	Number & Operations-Fractions	Understand a fraction 1/b as the quantity formed by 1 part when a whole is partitioned into b equal parts.
20	D	Measurement & Data	Tell and write time to the nearest minute and measure time intervals in minutes.

Q11.
110, 90, 280, 980, 860, 200, 40, 770

The student should provide an explanation that refers to considering the number in the ones place. The answer should include that the number is rounded down if the number is less than 5 and rounded up if the number is 5 or higher.

Scoring Information
Give a total score out of 4.
Give a score of 0.25 for each number correctly rounded.
Give a score out of 2 for the explanation.

Q13.
The two models should have shaded 3 of the 10 segments and 2 of the 10 segments.
The > symbol should be placed in the empty box.

The student may explain how shading the models allows the two fractions to be compared by seeing how many parts of 10 each fraction is. The student may explain how you can compare the fractions as parts of the same whole.

Scoring Information
Give a total score out of 4.
Give a score of 1 for each correct shading.
Give a score of 1 for the correct symbol.
Give a score out of 2 for the explanation.

Q14.
Expression: $x + 3$
Answer: 34
Answer: 115

Scoring Information
Give a total score out of 3.
Give a score of 1 for the correct expression.
Give a score of 1 for each correct answer.

Q15.
$6 \times 5 = 30$, then $30 \times 3 = 90$ OR $5 \times 6 = 30$, then $30 \times 3 = 90$
$6 \times 3 = 18$, then $18 \times 5 = 90$ OR $3 \times 6 = 18$, then $18 \times 5 = 90$
$5 \times 3 = 15$, then $15 \times 6 = 90$ OR $3 \times 5 = 15$, then $15 \times 6 = 90$

Scoring Information
Give a total score out of 3.
Give a score of 1 for each correct number sentence.

SBAC Mathematics, Practice Set 4

Question	Answer	Topic	Common Core State Standard
1	A	Geometry	Partition shapes into parts with equal areas. Express the area of each part as a unit fraction of the whole.
2	A	Operations/Algebraic Thinking	Understand division as an unknown-factor problem.
3	B	Measurement & Data	Recognize area as an attribute of plane figures and understand concepts of area measurement, including that a plane figure which can be covered without gaps or overlaps by *n* unit squares is said to have an area of *n* square units.
4	1st and 2nd	Geometry	Understand that shapes in different categories may share attribute, and that the shared attributes can define a larger category (e.g., quadrilaterals).
5	B	Measurement & Data	Measure and estimate masses of objects.
6	D	Operations/Algebraic Thinking	Identify arithmetic patterns, and explain them using properties of operations.
7	16 cans	Measurement & Data	Draw a scaled picture graph to represent a data set with several categories.
8	C	Measurement & Data	Solve real world and mathematical problems involving perimeters of polygons, including finding the perimeter given the side lengths.
9	75, 90, 105	Operations/Algebraic Thinking	Identify arithmetic patterns, and explain them using properties of operations.
10	C	Number & Operations-Fractions	Understand a fraction 1/*b* as the quantity formed by 1 part when *a* whole is partitioned into *b* equal parts; understand a fraction *a*/*b* as the quantity formed by *a* parts of size 1/*b*.
11	See Below	Number & Operations in Base Ten	Use place value understanding to round whole numbers to the nearest 10 or 100.
12	$6	Operations/Algebraic Thinking	Use multiplication and division within 100 to solve word problems in situations involving equal groups, arrays, and measurement quantities.
13	91 minutes	Measurement & Data	Tell and write time to the nearest minute and measure time intervals in minutes. Solve word problems involving addition and subtraction of time intervals in minutes.
14	See Below	Number & Operations-Fractions	Recognize and generate simple equivalent fractions. Explain why the fractions are equivalent, e.g., by using a visual fraction model.
15	See Below	Measurement & Data	Solve mathematical problems involving perimeters of polygons, including exhibiting rectangles with the same perimeter and different areas or with the same area and different perimeters.
16	B	Measurement & Data	Draw a scaled picture graph to represent a data set with several categories.
17	D	Operations/Algebraic Thinking	Solve two-step word problems using the four operations.
18	$575	Number & Operations in Base Ten	Fluently add and subtract within 1000 using strategies and algorithms based on place value, properties of operations, and/or the relationship between addition and subtraction.
19	B	Operations/Algebraic Thinking	Fluently multiply and divide within 100. Know from memory all products of two one-digit numbers.
20	A	Measurement & Data	Solve real world and mathematical problems involving perimeters of polygons, including finding the perimeter given the side lengths.

Q11.
Nearest ten: 8,780
Nearest hundred: 8,800

The student should provide an explanation that refers to considering the number in the ones place when rounding to the nearest ten and considering the number in the tens place when rounding to the nearest hundred. The answer should include that the number is rounded down if the number is less than 5 and rounded up if the number is 5 or higher.

Scoring Information
Give a total score out of 4.
Give a score of 1 for each correct rounding.
Give a score out of 2 for the explanation.

Q14.
The halves fraction bar should have 1 of the 2 segments shaded.
The quarters fraction bar should have 2 of the 4 segments shaded.
The eighths fraction bar should have 4 of the 8 segments shaded.
Fraction: $\frac{4}{8}$

Scoring Information
Give a total score out of 4.
Give a score of 1 for each fraction bar correctly shaded.
Give a score of 1 for the correct fraction.

Q15.
18 square units
The grid should have a 6 by 3 rectangle drawn on it.

Scoring Information
Give a total score out of 3.
Give a score of 1 for the correct area.
Give a score of 2 for a 6 by 3 rectangle.
Give a score of 1 for a non-rectangular shape with an area of 18 square units.

SBAC Mathematics, Practice Set 5

Question	Answer	Topic	Common Core State Standard
1	C	Measurement & Data	Recognize perimeter as an attribute of plane figures and distinguish between linear and area measures.
2	D	Measurement & Data	Multiply side lengths to find areas of rectangles with whole-number side lengths in the context of solving real world and mathematical problems.
3	3rd and 4th	Operations/Algebraic Thinking	Solve two-step word problems using the four operations.
4	1,300 1,290	Number & Operations in Base Ten	Use place value understanding to round whole numbers to the nearest 10 or 100.
5	C	Operations/Algebraic Thinking	Interpret whole-number quotients of whole numbers, e.g., interpret 56 ÷ 8 as the number of objects in each share when 56 objects are partitioned equally into 8 shares.
6	A	Operations/Algebraic Thinking	Solve two-step word problems using the four operations.
7	A	Measurement & Data	Recognize area as an attribute of plane figures and understand concepts of area measurement, including that a plane figure which can be covered without gaps or overlaps by *n* unit squares is said to have an area of *n* square units.
8	C	Operations/Algebraic Thinking	Assess the reasonableness of answers using mental computation and estimation strategies including rounding.
9	C	Operations/Algebraic Thinking	Interpret products of whole numbers and whole-number quotients of whole numbers.
10	1, 0	Operations/Algebraic Thinking	Determine the unknown whole number in a multiplication or division equation relating three whole numbers.
11	4 miles Ryan and Leah 6 miles	Measurement & Data	Solve one- and two-step "how many more" and "how many less" problems using information presented in scaled bar graphs.
12	B	Measurement & Data	Recognize area as an attribute of plane figures and understand concepts of area measurement.
13	B	Number & Operations in Base Ten	Use place value understanding to round whole numbers to the nearest 10 or 100.
14	$\frac{2}{6}$ and $\frac{1}{3}$	Number & Operations-Fractions	Recognize and generate simple equivalent fractions. Explain why the fractions are equivalent, e.g., by using a visual fraction model.
15	C	Operations/Algebraic Thinking	Interpret products of whole numbers, e.g., interpret 5 × 7 as the total number of objects in 5 groups of 7 objects each.
16	Point at $2\frac{3}{4}$	Number & Operations-Fractions	Understand a fraction as a number on the number line; represent fractions on a number line diagram.
17	Red $\frac{1}{4}$ Green $\frac{1}{2}$ Blue $\frac{1}{10}$ White $\frac{3}{20}$	Number & Operations-Fractions	Understand a fraction 1/*b* as the quantity formed by 1 part when *a* whole is partitioned into *b* equal parts; understand a fraction *a*/*b* as the quantity formed by *a* parts of size 1/*b*.
18	24 pieces of pie	Operations/Algebraic Thinking	Use multiplication and division within 100 to solve word problems in situations involving equal groups.
19	$\frac{1}{8}, \frac{1}{4}, \frac{3}{10}$	Number & Operations-Fractions	Compare two fractions with the same numerator or the same denominator by reasoning about their size.
20	150 + 150 + 50 + 50 = 400 2(150 + 50) = 400	Measurement & Data	Solve real world and mathematical problems involving perimeters of polygons.

SBAC Mathematics, Practice Set 6

Question	Answer	Topic	Common Core State Standard
1	A	Geometry	Partition shapes into parts with equal areas.
2	D	Operations/Algebraic Thinking	Apply properties of operations as strategies to multiply and divide.
3	$3 50 muffins	Operations/Algebraic Thinking	Identify arithmetic patterns, and explain them using properties of operations.
4	36 cm²	Measurement & Data	Multiply side lengths to find areas of rectangles with whole-number side lengths in the context of solving real world and mathematical problems.
5	A	Operations/Algebraic Thinking	Represent problems using equations with a letter standing for the unknown quantity.
6	D	Operations/Algebraic Thinking	Solve two-step word problems using the four operations.
7	Tuesday 13° 9°	Measurement & Data	Solve one- and two-step "how many more" and "how many less" problems using information presented in scaled bar graphs.
8	Any 3 of the 4 squares shaded, $\frac{3}{4}$	Number & Operations-Fractions	Recognize and generate simple equivalent fractions. Explain why the fractions are equivalent, e.g., by using a visual fraction model.
9	1st and 6th	Operations/Algebraic Thinking	Use multiplication and division within 100 to solve word problems in situations involving equal groups, arrays, and measurement quantities.
10	D	Operations/Algebraic Thinking	Represent problems using equations with a letter standing for the unknown quantity.
11	B	Measurement & Data	Solve one- and two-step "how many more" and "how many less" problems using information presented in scaled bar graphs.
12	B	Measurement & Data	Draw a scaled picture graph to represent a data set with several categories.
13	16, 32, 40	Operations/Algebraic Thinking	Use multiplication and division within 100 to solve word problems in situations involving equal groups, arrays, and measurement quantities.
14	24, 28	Operations/Algebraic Thinking	Identify arithmetic patterns, and explain them using properties of operations.
15	A	Number & Operations-Fractions	Understand a fraction 1/*b* as the quantity formed by 1 part when *a* whole is partitioned into *b* equal parts; understand a fraction *a*/*b* as the quantity formed by *a* parts of size 1/*b*.
16	A	Number & Operations-Fractions	Recognize and generate simple equivalent fractions. Explain why the fractions are equivalent, e.g., by using a visual fraction model.
17	$\frac{2}{5}$	Number & Operations-Fractions	Understand a fraction 1/*b* as the quantity formed by 1 part when *a* whole is partitioned into *b* equal parts.
18	C	Measurement & Data	Measure and estimate liquid volumes.
19	C	Number & Operations in Base Ten	Fluently add and subtract within 1000 using strategies and algorithms.
20	B	Measurement & Data	Measure and estimate liquid volumes and masses of objects using standard units of grams (g), kilograms (kg), and liters (l). Add, subtract, multiply, or divide to solve one-step word problems involving masses or volumes that are given in the same units.

SBAC Mathematics, Practice Set 7

Question	Answer	Topic	Common Core State Standard
1	B	Number & Operations in Base Ten	Multiply one-digit whole numbers by multiples of 10 in the range 10–90 using strategies based on place value and properties of operations.
2	204	Number & Operations in Base Ten	Fluently add and subtract within 1000 using strategies and algorithms based on place value, properties of operations, and/or the relationship between addition and subtraction.
3	35,682 62,854	Number & Operations in Base Ten	Use place value understanding to round whole numbers to the nearest 10 or 100.
4	D	Operations/Algebraic Thinking	Interpret whole-number quotients of whole numbers, e.g., interpret 56 ÷ 8 as the number of objects in each share when 56 objects are partitioned equally into 8 shares, or as a number of shares when 56 objects are partitioned into equal shares of 8 objects each.
5	Any 3 of the 9 stars shaded	Number & Operations-Fractions	Understand a fraction 1/b as the quantity formed by 1 part when a whole is partitioned into b equal parts; understand a fraction a/b as the quantity formed by a parts of size 1/b.
6	D	Measurement & Data	Multiply side lengths to find areas of rectangles with whole-number side lengths in the context of solving real world and mathematical problems.
7	A	Measurement & Data	Find areas of rectilinear figures by decomposing them into non-overlapping rectangles and adding the areas of the non-overlapping parts.
8	C	Operations/Algebraic Thinking	Assess the reasonableness of answers using mental computation and estimation strategies including rounding.
9	C	Geometry	Understand that shapes in different categories (e.g., rhombuses, rectangles, and others) may share attributes (e.g., having four sides), and that the shared attributes can define a larger category (e.g., quadrilaterals). Recognize rhombuses, rectangles, and squares as examples of quadrilaterals.
10	9 cm	Measurement & Data	Solve real world and mathematical problems involving perimeters of polygons, including finding an unknown side length.
11	$\frac{1}{4}$ of the customers	Number & Operations-Fractions	Understand a fraction 1/b as the quantity formed by 1 part when a whole is partitioned into b equal parts; understand a fraction a/b as the quantity formed by a parts of size 1/b.
12	128	Operations/Algebraic Thinking	Identify arithmetic patterns, and explain them using properties of operations.
13	3:45 p.m.	Measurement & Data	Tell and write time to the nearest minute and measure time intervals in minutes. Solve word problems involving addition and subtraction of time intervals in minutes.
14	480	Number & Operations in Base Ten	Multiply one-digit whole numbers by multiples of 10 in the range 10–90 using strategies based on place value and properties of operations.

15	12 miles	Number & Operations in Base Ten	Fluently add and subtract within 1000 using strategies and algorithms based on place value, properties of operations, and/or the relationship between addition and subtraction.
16	Bar to 9 Bar to 5 2 players	Measurement & Data	Draw a scaled bar graph to represent a data set with several categories. Solve one- and two-step "how many more" and "how many less" problems using information presented in scaled bar graphs.
17	See Below	Geometry	Understand that shapes in different categories (e.g., rhombuses, rectangles, and others) may share attributes (e.g., having four sides), and that the shared attributes can define a larger category (e.g., quadrilaterals).
18	See Below	Geometry	Partition shapes into parts with equal areas. Express the area of each part as a unit fraction of the whole.
19	12 square feet 14 feet	Measurement & Data	Solve real world and mathematical problems involving areas and perimeters of rectangles.
20	See Below	Geometry	Understand that shapes in different categories may share attributes, and that the shared attributes can define a larger category.

Q17.
The rhombus, the trapezoid, and the rectangle should be circled.
The property identified could be that all the shapes have four sides or that all the shapes have four angles.

Scoring Information
Give a total score out of 4.
Give a score of 1 for each shape correctly circled. Take off 1 point for each additional shape incorrectly circled.
Give a score out of 1 for the explanation.

Q18.
The student should divide the hexagon into 6 equal triangles, as shown below.

Answer: $\frac{1}{3}$ or $\frac{2}{6}$

Scoring Information
Give a total score out of 2.
Give a score of 1 for a correct division into 6 equal triangles.
Give a score of 1 for the correct answer.

Q20.
The rhombus in the center should be circled.
Answers may describe any two of the following similarities:
    They both have 4 sides or 4 equal sides.   They both have 4 angles.
    They both have congruent or equal sides.   They both have parallel sides.

Scoring Information
Give a total score out of 3.
Give a score of 1 for the correct shape circled.
Give a score of 1 for each similarity correctly described.

SBAC Mathematics, Practice Set 8

Question	Answer	Topic	Common Core State Standard
1	D	Number & Operations-Fractions	Understand a fraction 1/b as the quantity formed by 1 part when a whole is partitioned into b equal parts; understand a fraction a/b as the quantity formed by a parts of size 1/b.
2	Eva, Leah	Measurement & Data	Solve one- and two-step "how many more" and "how many less" problems using information presented in scaled bar graphs.
3	B	Operations/Algebraic Thinking	Solve two-step word problems using the four operations.
4	27 ÷ 3 = 9 27 ÷ 9 = 3	Operations/Algebraic Thinking	Interpret whole-number quotients of whole numbers, e.g., interpret 56 ÷ 8 as the number of objects in each share when 56 objects are partitioned equally into 8 shares.
5	1st and 4th	Measurement & Data	Find areas of rectilinear figures by decomposing them into non-overlapping rectangles and adding the areas of the non-overlapping parts.
6	C	Operations/Algebraic Thinking	Solve two-step word problems using the four operations.
7	B	Operations/Algebraic Thinking	Identify arithmetic patterns, and explain them using properties of operations.
8	C	Operations/Algebraic Thinking	Assess the reasonableness of answers using mental computation and estimation strategies including rounding.
9	4 trees	Measurement & Data	Solve one- and two-step "how many more" and "how many less" problems using information presented in scaled bar graphs.
10	B	Operations/Algebraic Thinking	Solve two-step word problems using the four operations.
11	6 + 5 + 6 + 5 = 22 2(6 + 5) = 22	Measurement & Data	Solve real world and mathematical problems involving perimeters of polygons, including finding the perimeter given the side lengths.
12	D	Geometry	Partition shapes into parts with equal areas. Express the area of each part as a unit fraction of the whole.
13	C	Operations/Algebraic Thinking	Fluently multiply and divide within 100. Know from memory all products of two one-digit numbers.
14	20, 30, 40	Number & Operations in Base Ten	Use place value understanding to round whole numbers to the nearest 10 or 100.
15	$\frac{2}{8} = \frac{1}{4}$	Number & Operations-Fractions	Recognize and generate simple equivalent fractions. Explain why the fractions are equivalent, e.g., by using a visual fraction model.
16	A	Number & Operations-Fractions	Understand a fraction as a number on the number line; represent fractions on a number line diagram.
17	B	Operations/Algebraic Thinking	Interpret products of whole numbers, e.g., interpret 5 × 7 as the total number of objects in 5 groups of 7 objects each.
18	8 pizzas	Operations/Algebraic Thinking	Use multiplication and division within 100 to solve word problems in situations involving equal groups, arrays, and measurement quantities.
19	40 ÷ 8 = 5 or 40 ÷ 5 = 8	Operations/Algebraic Thinking	Fluently multiply and divide within 100, using strategies such as the relationship between multiplication and division or properties of operations.
20	C	Measurement & Data	Measure and estimate masses of objects.

SBAC Mathematics, Practice Set 9

Question	Answer	Topic	Common Core State Standard
1	D	Measurement & Data	Solve real world and mathematical problems involving perimeters of polygons, including finding the perimeter given the side lengths.
2	36	Operations/Algebraic Thinking	Identify arithmetic patterns, and explain them using properties of operations.
3	C	Geometry	Recognize rhombuses, rectangles, and squares as examples of quadrilaterals.
4	C	Operations/Algebraic Thinking	Identify arithmetic patterns, and explain them using properties of operations.
5	A	Operations/Algebraic Thinking	Apply properties of operations as strategies to multiply and divide, including the distributive property.
6	2nd and 4th	Operations/Algebraic Thinking	Use multiplication and division within 100 to solve word problems in situations involving equal groups, arrays, and measurement quantities.
7	8 emails	Measurement & Data	Draw a scaled picture graph to represent a data set with several categories.
8	B	Measurement & Data	Tell and write time to the nearest minute and measure time intervals in minutes.
9	D	Measurement & Data	Multiply side lengths to find areas of rectangles with whole-number side lengths in the context of solving real world and mathematical problems.
10	A	Measurement & Data	Draw a scaled picture graph to represent a data set with several categories.
11	C	Measurement & Data	Add, subtract, multiply, or divide to solve one-step word problems involving masses or volumes that are given in the same units.
12	Any 2 of the 8 squares shaded	Number & Operations-Fractions	Recognize and generate simple equivalent fractions. Explain why the fractions are equivalent, e.g., by using a visual fraction model.
13	336 students	Operations/Algebraic Thinking	Fluently multiply and divide within 100, using strategies such as the relationship between multiplication and division or properties of operations.
14	B	Measurement & Data	Generate measurement data by measuring lengths using rulers marked with halves and fourths of an inch.
15	C	Operations/Algebraic Thinking	Understand division as an unknown-factor problem.
16	B	Measurement & Data	Tell and write time to the nearest minute and measure time intervals in minutes.
17	A	Number & Operations-Fractions	Record the results of comparisons with the symbols >, =, or <, and justify the conclusions, e.g., by using a visual fraction model.
18	C	Operations/Algebraic Thinking	Interpret products of whole numbers, e.g., interpret 5 × 7 as the total number of objects in 5 groups of 7 objects each.
19	10, 14, 28	Operations/Algebraic Thinking	Use multiplication and division within 100 to solve word problems in situations involving equal groups, arrays, and measurement quantities.
20	20, 32, 44	Operations/Algebraic Thinking	Interpret products of whole numbers, e.g., interpret 5 × 7 as the total number of objects in 5 groups of 7 objects each.

SBAC Mathematics, Practice Set 10

Question	Answer	Topic	Common Core State Standard
1	B	Operations/Algebraic Thinking	Solve two-step word problems using the four operations.
2	2, 3, 1, 4	Number & Operations-Fractions	Compare two fractions with the same numerator or the same denominator by reasoning about their size.
3	A	Operations/Algebraic Thinking	Use multiplication and division within 100 to solve word problems in situations involving equal groups, arrays, and measurement quantities.
4	C	Operations/Algebraic Thinking	Solve two-step word problems using the four operations.
5	$\frac{4}{2}, \frac{8}{4}$	Number & Operations-Fractions	Express whole numbers as fractions, and recognize fractions that are equivalent to whole numbers.
6	D	Measurement & Data	Draw a scaled picture graph to represent a data set with several categories.
7	$\frac{3}{6}$ and $\frac{6}{12}$	Number & Operations-Fractions	Recognize and generate simple equivalent fractions.
8	Dean: kite Selma: triangle	Geometry	Understand that shapes in different categories (e.g., rhombuses, rectangles, and others) may share attributes (e.g., having four sides), and that the shared attributes can define a larger category (e.g., quadrilaterals).
9	B	Measurement & Data	Solve real world and mathematical problems involving perimeters of polygons, including finding the perimeter given the side lengths.
10	C	Measurement & Data	Measure and estimate masses of objects.
11	See Below	Number & Operations in Base Ten	Use place value understanding to round whole numbers to the nearest 10 or 100.
12	48, 54, 60	Operations/Algebraic Thinking	Identify arithmetic patterns, and explain them using properties of operations.
13	5 years	Operations/Algebraic Thinking	Use multiplication and division within 100 to solve word problems in situations involving equal groups, arrays, and measurement quantities.
14	21 square centimeters	Measurement & Data	Recognize area as an attribute of plane figures and understand concepts of area measurement, including that a plane figure which can be covered without gaps or overlaps by n unit squares is said to have an area of n square units.
15	17 customers	Number & Operations in Base Ten	Fluently add and subtract within 1000 using strategies and algorithms based on place value, properties of operations, and/or the relationship between addition and subtraction.
16	Jan: bar to 18 Feb: bar to 16 Mar: Bar to 14 $5	Measurement & Data	Draw a scaled bar graph to represent a data set with several categories. Solve one- and two-step "how many more" and "how many less" problems using information presented in scaled bar graphs.
17	See Below	Operations/Algebraic Thinking	Identify arithmetic patterns, and explain them using properties of operations.
18	$532	Measurement & Data	Solve real world and mathematical problems involving perimeters of polygons, including finding the perimeter given the side lengths.
19	See Below	Number & Operations-Fractions	Recognize and generate simple equivalent fractions. Explain why the fractions are equivalent, e.g., by using a visual fraction model.

| 20 | See Below | Number & Operations in Base Ten | Recognize that in a multi-digit whole number, a digit in one place represents ten times what it represents in the place to its right. Compare two multi-digit numbers based on meanings of the digits in each place. |

Q11.
The number 48 should be plotted on the number line.
Answer: 50
The student should explain how you can tell that the number is closer to 50 than 40.

Scoring Information
Give a total score out of 3.
Give a score of 1 for the number correctly plotted on the number line.
Give a score of 1 for rounding the number correctly.
Give a score out of 1 for the explanation.

Q17.
Answer: 25

The explanation should describe how each number in the pattern is 3 more than the number before it, and that the next number is found by adding 3 to 22.

Scoring Information
Give a total score out of 3.
Give a score of 1 for the correct answer.
Give a score out of 2 for the explanation.

Q19.
The model should have 3 parts of 18 shaded, or 1 part of 6 shaded, as shown below.

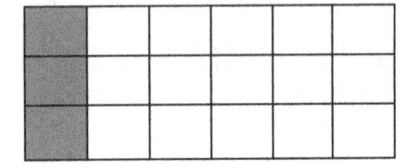

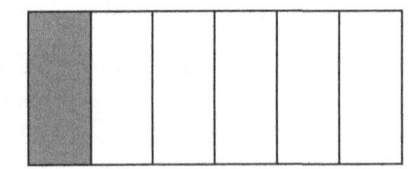

Answer: $\frac{1}{6}$

Scoring Information
Give a total score out of 3.
Give a score of 2 for the correct shading.
Give a score of 1 for the correct answer.

Q20.
146 and 164

The explanation should refer to the place value of the numbers. It may describe how the number with the lowest value should be in the hundreds place.

Scoring Information
Give a total score out of 4.
Give a score of 1 for each correct number.
Give a score out of 2 for the explanation.

Get to Know Our Product Range

Mathematics

Practice Test Books
Practice sets and practice tests will prepare students for the state tests.

Common Core Quiz Books
Focused individual quizzes cover every math skill one by one.

English Language Arts/Reading

Practice Test Books
Practice sets and practice tests will prepare students for the state tests.

Reading Skills Workbooks
Short passages and question sets will develop and improve reading comprehension skills and are perfect for ongoing test prep.

Writing

Writing Skills Workbooks
Students write narratives, essays, and opinion pieces, and write in response to passages.

Persuasive and Narrative Writing Workbooks
Guided workbooks teach all the skills needed to write narratives and opinion pieces.

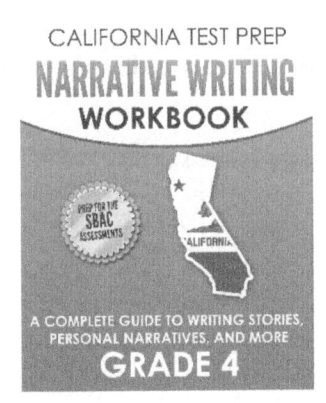

Language and Vocabulary

Language and Vocabulary Quiz Books
Focused quizzes cover spelling, grammar, usage, writing conventions, and vocabulary.

Revising and Editing Workbooks
Students improve language skills and writing skills by identifying and correcting errors.

Language Skills Workbooks
Exercises on specific language skills including figurative language, synonyms, and homographs.

http://www.testmasterpress.com

Made in the USA
Middletown, DE
07 January 2025